Cheap Thrills Montreal

[2006]

## OTHER TITLES IN THE SERIES

Cheap Thrills Toronto

Cheap Thrills New York

# Cheap Thrills
## MONTREAL

Great Montreal Meals
for under $ 15.00

[2006]

Nancy Marrelli
& Simon Dardick

Véhicule Press

Véhicule Press acknowledges the support of the Government of Canada's Book Industry Development Program

Cover illustration: Béatrice Favereau
Cover art direction and design: JW Stewart
Special thanks to Vicki Marcok and Stephanie MacLean
Inside imaging: Simon Garamond
Printing: Marquis Book Printing Inc.

CATALOGUING IN PUBLICATION DATA

Cheap thrills Montreal : great Montreal meals
for under $15 / Nancy Marrelli & Simon Dardick

ISBN 1-55065-183-8

1. Restaurants–Quebec(Province)–Montreal–Guidebooks.
I. Marrelli, Nancy. II. Dardick, Simon, 1943-

TX907.5 C22M6 2005    647.95714'28    C2004-90002-0

Published by Véhicule Press
P.O.B. 125, Place du Parc Station
Montréal, Québec  H2X 4A3

514.844.6073    FAX 514.844.7543

www.vehiculepress.com
www.cheapthrillsguides.com

CANADIAN DISTRIBUTION
LPG Distribution Collective
800-591-6250

U.S. DISTRIBUTION
Independent Publishers Group, Chicago, Illinois
800-888-4741

Printed in Canada

# Contents

What is a Cheap Thrill? 6

Our Reviewers 7

Introduction 9

Alphabetical List of Restaurants 11

Cheap Thrills @ Lunch 15

Reviews 19

The Sex of Restaurants 110

Specialty Index 113

Neighbourhood Index 117

## What is a Cheap Thrill?

The restaurants in this book generally offer meals at dinner for $15 or less. This does not mean that every meal in the restaurant will be under $15, but there should be a reasonable selection in that price range before taxes, tip, and alcohol.

## Independent Reviews

We pride ourselves on the independence of our reviews. No offers of free food or any other gratuities are ever accepted by our reviewers.

## Check It Out Before You Go

Restaurants change constantly—menus, hours, and owners are in constant flux. The information in this book was current at the time of publication, but there's no guarantee that things won't change without warning. It's a good idea to call ahead.

# Our Reviewers

Joanne Alfieri
Chris Anderson
Kiki Athanassiadis
Sach Baylin-Stern
Emily Beauregard
John Beaugregard
Howard Bokser
Elise Boyer
Meredith Carruthers
Ann Charney
Melvin Charney
Denis Chouinard
Josh Cuppage
Anne Dardick
Rosemary Dardick
Karin Derouaux
Sarah Dick
David Engle
Marif Flores
Tess Fragoulis
Kim Fraser
Pietro Gasparrini
Anne Greengrove
Bruce Henry
Alan Hustak
Alison Judd
Jon Kalina
Sikeena Karmali
Meghan Kelley
Nicole Kennedy
Barry Lazar
Jillian Logan

Stephanie MacLean
Vicki Marcok
Lissa Matyas
Scott McRae
Joan McSheffrey
Leslie Orr
Colin Pearson
Christian Pronovost
Tom Puchniak
Linda Ramsay
Rossitza Ribabova
Tommy Schnurmacher
Jaspreet Singh
Alex Smith
Carmine Starnino
Carole Welp
Fabien Welp-Barr
John Wilkinson
Janis Zubalik

# Introduction

This book is about eating out well in Montreal.

People *love* to eat out in this incredible food city. You can eat your way through many cultures and cuisines, and you can do it to fit almost any pocketbook. These days we eat out for many reasons: we're too busy or frazzled to cook every day, we want to try something new, or we prefer to share a meal with friends or family without doing the cooking or the cleanup! We look for affordable pleasure, a congenial atmosphere, and a little adventure.

*Cheap Thrills Montreal* explores many corners of a fascinating city in search of good food at reasonable prices. The roots of Montrealers run long and deep and our collective past is vibrantly reflected in what we love to eat—Montreal's own homegrown specialties as well as food traditions from the rainbow mix of people who live here.

This is the fifth edition of a book that set out to discover Montrealers' favourite inexpensive restaurants. We update our "classics" but we also search out new places and different neighbourhoods to keep pace with rising costs and fresh discoveries. Of course the food has to be excellent, not just cheap! The food scene constantly changes and over the years the mix of what's available and where has shifted. This is partly due to changing patterns of newly-arrived immigrants who venture into the restaurant business, and the neighbourhoods in which people live and eat. A wide variety of people bring us their latest and best finds. The list of reviewers and contributors is in the front of the book: we thank them all for their good appetite, judgement, and willingness to share their discoveries with us all.

A "cheap thrill" is $15 or less for dinner, before taxes, tip, and alcohol. Many of our selections are below the limit and a few are hugging the top. We've added a new feature—*Cheap Thrills @ Lunch*. These are places that are either open only at lunch or their price range is within the Cheap Thrills limit only at lunchtime. We hope you find it useful. We're also doing more on our website—visit us at www.cheapthrillsguides.com.

*Cheap Thrills* is a celebration of the wonderful food available in Montreal, and the diverse cultures that have been interwoven into the fabric of this beautiful old North American city. We are fortunate to share this diversity. *Cheap Thrills Montreal* will take you around the city and around the world.

This is how Montreal eats!

# Alphabetical List of Restaurants

Agostini 19
Al Mandy 20
Amelio's 21
Arirang 22
Arzou Express 23
Aux Vivres 24

B&M 25
Ban Lao Thai 26
Bangkok 27
Banquise, La 28
Barroso Grill 29
Beniamino & Co. 30
Binerie Mont-Royal, La 31
Bistro Gourmet 2 15
Bistro San Lucas 32
Bo 15
Boîte à Lunch 33
Bombay Choupati 34
Bombay Mahal 35
Braseiro 36
Brodino 15
Buffet Palace Oriental 37

Cabane, La 38
Café International 39
Café L'Étranger 40
Café Rococo 41
Café Titanic 16
Caffe Grazie Mille 42
Caraibe Delite 43
Caverne, Le 44

Chalet Bar B-Q 45
Chez Badi 46
Chez Benny 47
Chez Bong (Chinatown) 48
Chez Bong (Downtown) 49
Chez Clo 16
Chilenita, La 50
Chino Soul 51
Chopin 16
Chuch 52
Cluny Artbar 16
Cobalt 53
Cracovie 54
Cuba 55

Diogènes 56

Exception, L' 57

Keur Fatou 58

L Corridor 59
L' Exception 57
La Banquise 28
La Binerie Mont-Royal 31
La Cabane 38
La Chilenita 50
La Nouba 75
Le Caverne 44
Le Grand Comptoir 17
Le Petit Verdun 80
Le Tropico 105
Les Gourmets Pressés 17
Lin et Lin 60
Lobby Bar 61

Lola Rosa 62
Los Planes Pupuseria 63

Ma's Place 64
Main, The 104
Maison du Bedouin 65
Maison du Kebab 66
Malhi Sweets 67
Maria Bonita 68
Marven's 69
Mazurka 70
MbCo 17
McKibbin's Irish Pub 71
Melchorita 72
Mexicasa 73

Nguyen Phi 74
Nouba, La 75

Olive & Gourmando 17
Om 76

Papa Khan 77
Perle de Manila 78
Persepolis 79
Petit Verdun, Le 80
Pharmacie Esperanza 81
Piment Fort 82
Pizza Cachère Pita 83
Pizza Villa 84
Prato 85
Première Moisson 86
Pushap 87

Quartier Perse 88
Quatre Saisons 89

Réservoir 18
Riccardo's 90
Roi du Plateau 91
Romados 92
Rotisserie Mavi 93
Royal Sous-marines 94
Royal Sushi 95

Sablo Kafé 96
Saffron 97
St-Viateur Bagel & Café 98
Santangelos Sandwicherie Italienne 99
Schwartz's 100
Shish-Kebab 101
Soy 18
Strega du Village 102

Tabaq 103
The Main 104
Tropico, Le 105

Vasco de Gama 106
Villa Wellington 107
Village Mon Nan 108

# Cheap Thrills @ Lunch

There are many places in this book that serve great lunches; these are a few additional recommendations. Some of the restos on this list are only open at lunchtime; others only meet the Cheap Thrills guidelines at noon, not at dinner ($15 before tax, wine, tip). But they're all great places to eat!

## Bistro Gourmet 2
**4007 St-Denis** (corner Duluth)
Phone: 514.844.0555
*Daily specials: $10.50+ at lunch; $17+ at night*
Bistro Gourmet 2 is the quintessential elegant French bistro with classic bistro food at a *prix fixe* starting at $10.50 at lunch, rising to $17+ at night. Portions are generous and presentation is done with flair and high style. There is a lovely outdoor terrace on St-Denis.

## Bo
**5163 St-Laurent** (near Fairmount)
Phone: 514.272.6886
*Asian wraps: $8.50; lunch table d'hôte: $10*
The newly-opened Bo (same talented owners as nearby Soy) in the old Ciné-Lumière has glorious Asian food. Lunch features Asian wraps with BBQ duck, sesame beef, and a table d'hôte. The exciting new menu reflects Chef Suzanne's usual panache. Dinner is available but is pricier.

## Brodino
**1049 Van Horne** (near Durocher)
Phone: 514.271.2229
Brodino is a small place with a select menu of soups, tempting sandwich combinations (some vegetarian) on a baguette or Kaiser bun, hot sandwiches and great burgers, plus desserts. They close at 3 pm.

## Café Titanic
**445 St-Pierre**
Phone: 514.849.0894
*Sandwiches: $3-$7.50; daily special: $12*
A bustling lunch place in Old Montreal with superb sandwiches on baguette or fougasse, quiche, salads, antipasto including great veggies, a daily special, and glorious desserts. Portions are generous and service is fast. They close at 4 pm.

## Chez Clo
**3199 Ontario E.** (at Dézéry)
Phone: 514.522.5348
*Average special: $8 (21 choices incl. soup, main, dessert, coffee)*
Chez Clo is a dynamite diner with old-time Québec comfort food. Breakfast is served all day. Food is unpretentious but satisfying and portions are hefty. They open very early and close mid-afternoon.

## Chopin
**4200 Décarie** (bet. Duquette & Brodeur)
Phone: 514.481.0302
*Sandwich: $3.39-$4.29; pierogi plate +salad $8*
Chopin is a Polish deli where light meals are served in a charming atmosphere. They serve homemade pierogi, hearty Polish soups, sandwiches made to order with the deli meats, cheesecake, and homemade seasonal desserts.

## Cluny Artbar
**257 Prince-William** (near Ottawa)
Phone: 514.866.1213
Cluny is in the exciting artist exhibition space, Quartier Ephémère. They serve light breakfast, sandwiches, soup, antipasto, and light dinners on Thursday and Friday evening. It's a beautifully-converted space in the old Darling foundry, run by the Café Titanic people.

## Le Grand Comptoir
**1225 Square Phillips** (near Ste-Catherine)
Phone: 514.393.3295
*Daily special: $12.95*
The daily special, like Toulouse sausages, (including soup and salad), is a bistro classic. The à la carte menu is $11-$19. A pleasant covered front terrace overlooks the square. They're very busy at lunch so get there early.

## Les Gourmets Pressés
**3911 St-Jacques W., St-Henri & 406 St-Jacques W.**
Phone: 514.937.6555 (St-Henri) / 514.842.5525
*Sandwich with salad, $10.*
Small, with hip décor—terrific sandwiches and salads, light meals, and chalkboard specials—all with nice touches and special house-made goodies. Breakfast and lunch available at both. "406" closes at 3 p.m. Dinner only available Thursday to Saturday at the St-Henri location, which closes at 7 p.m.

## MbCo (Montreal Bakery Company)
**1447 Stanley** (near de Maisonneuve) and other locations
514.284.040
*Sandwiches: $9*
An upscale sandwich place that serves sylish sandwiches and salads made with miso-glazed roasted salmon and chicken scaloppini with caramelized leeks etc. They also do breakfast. It's part of a restaurant group that's expanding.

## Olive & Gourmando
**351 St-Paul W.** (at St-Pierre)
Phone: 514.350.1083
*Sandwiches: $8.50*
Old Montreal bakery popular for breakfast and lunch, serving a limited menu of excellent fresh sandwiches, charcuterie and cheeses, salad, light daily specials, fantastic baked goods and Illy coffee. Open only Thursday for dinner, serving grilled fish and chicken.

## Réservoir
**9 Duluth E.** (near St-Laurent)
Phone: 514.849.7779
*Average daily lunch special: $15*
Le Réservoir is a brew-pub offering gastronomic delights at lunch. The menu changes daily with creative bistro-style food, using fresh ingredients. They serve only snacks in the evening. Their own beer is good too—cheap and delicious!

## Soy
**5258 St-Laurent** (at Fairmount)
Phone: 514.499.9399
*Midi-Express: $6.50; lunch table d'hote: $8.50-$14.50*
Soy is stylish, modern, casual, with spectacular food. Lunch specials include egg noodle dishes, General Tao chicken with subtle ginger/lemon flavour, sesame-peanut noodles with tofu, and Szechuan duck pancakes. Evening meals are beyond the *Cheap Thrills* limit.

# Agostini

**5545 Upper Lachine Rd.** (near Girouard)
Métro: Vendôme, then 90 or 104 bus
Phone: 514.485.0235
Hours: Mon-Sat 11am-9pm; closed Sunday
Credit cards: cash only; Alcohol: all
Wheelchair access: yes
*Daily special table d'hôte: $9-$9.95 (prices include tax)*

Agostini is a home-style Italian restaurant.

Specials of the day include homemade soup (pea soup on Fridays), a choice from three main courses such as lasagna, roast pork or chicken, salmon steak, and linguini with clams. It's one of the best deals in town. The regular menu includes pasta and veal specialties, pizza, and wonderful Italian submarine sandwiches. You could become addicted to their sausage sub: a crusty bun brimming with a juicy browned split Italian sausage, smothered with onions fried to melting perfection, tomato, and coleslaw or lettuce—it's a messy delight. You can pig out with the 14-inch but the 7-inch (optional double sausage) is enough for most people. "Some like it hot" and if you do be sure to top it all off with the zingy hot pepper sauce—so popular they sell containers to take out! Fries are fresh cut and delicious. Fresh fruit is a good dessert choice. Smooth espresso and cappuccino are excellent. They do take-out and deliver in this old Italian neighbourhood. All prices include taxes. It's tried and true rather than adventurous, but the food is unfailingly good.

Agostini is pleasant and bright but not plush. Children are welcome and service is friendly and efficient, although it's hectic at lunch. This is the kind of good food an Italian mom might make. Maria and Ezio Agostini arrived from Italy (Marche and Naples) in the late 1950s; their son Mario now owns the place but they, and daughter Antoinetta, are still very much part of the place. There's enough homemade good food to be able to eat here almost every day—and some locals do just that!

# Al Mandy

**1238 Mackay** (Ste-Catherine)
Métro: Guy-Concordia, or 15 bus
Phone: 514.223.3311
Hours: Mon-Thurs noon-10pm; Friday 2 pm-11pm; Sat 1pm-
  11pm; Sun 3pm-11pm
Credit cards: cash only; Alcohol: no
Wheelchair access: no
*Average main course: $7*

Al Mandy is a new place that is modestly introducing Yemeni cooking to downtown Montreal.

The menu is still small but new dishes are added as they go along. Everything is halal, and food is complemented by optional yogurt and a mild, tasty homemade sauce. Mandy lamb is wonderful—tender, savoury lamb on a bed of rice. Lamb koozy is a variation with added pasta, raisins, and a fresh tomato-based sauce. White or whole wheat *sabayah* is used to scoop up food or as a sandwich wrap for chicken or beef. Complex spices (not hot) are used on the spicy chicken. The Yemeni-style samosas (vegetarian, tuna, chicken, or beef) make a crispy snack in a thin wrapper. Fish and chips or chicken with rice are also available and can be adorned with sauce and yogurt. Kingfish with rice, veal mandy and honey-laced masoub are coming soon. A special soup to end the fast is served during Ramadan. Pass on the frozen fries, and be sure to ask for the special Yemeni salad dressing. They do catering and takeout.

Yemenis Ahmed Subain and son Mohammed opened this small place early in 2004. It is pretty basic, with desert murals and tables on a small flagstone terrace out front. Yemen is the size of the Yukon, with a long coastline and unforgiving geography: rugged mountains, desert, and little arable land (vegetables are not prominent here). In the Gulf States Yemeni cooking is highly regarded, known for its use of turmeric, fenugreek, cardamom, coriander and other spices. Food is eaten with the hands or with a spoon and fork; no knives. They are very helpful and proud to introduce Yemeni food traditions to Montreal.

# Amelio's

**201 Milton** (at Ste-Famille)
Métro: Place-des Arts and/or 80 bus
Phone: 514.845.8396
Hours: Mon-Sat 4pm-9pm; Tues-Fri 1:30 am-9pm; closed Sunday
Credit cards: cash only; Alcohol: BYOB
Wheelchair access: no
*Average main course: $8*

Amelio's serves some of Montreal's best thick crust pizza, at very affordable prices.

Along with this great pizza, Amelio's also has a wide range of pasta dishes and submarines. Reduced fat cheese is an option for most dishes. All the expected pizza toppings are available and they're fresh, but also on offer is ground Italian sausage, ham, ground beef, and feta cheese. The spicing and pizza sauce are perfect and the crust (white or whole wheat) is excellent. The salad that arrives with the pizza is standard lettuce, carrots, and onions with a good vinaigrette but it complements the pizza nicely. The garlic bread is fresh and hot and is available with or without cheese. Pastas are available with tomato, meat, rosé, vegetarian, or pesto sauce. The baked lasagna or manicotti are top notch, and the subs are good too. But somehow Amelio's is really about the yummy pizza—the crust and the sauce are perfect complements to your choice of toppings.

Amelio's is not about chic décor. It's a small plain space with café-style chairs, a brick wall, a window onto Ste-Famille—and no trendy decoration. It's as comfortable as well-worn jeans, and it will seem familiar even if it's your first visit. It's a popular spot for students and families and it gets very crowded and noisy on weekends—but always amiably so. Service is efficient and practiced, but not rushed or overbearing. Amelio opened here in 1985 when his career in banking ended. He took his pizza-making hobby to a new level and has been serving happy customers without interruption. Way to go Amelio! We're glad you switched!

# Arirang

**1858 Ste-Catherine W.** (near St-Marc)
Métro: Guy-Concordia or 15 bus
Phone: 514.846.0944
Hours: Mon-Sat 11am-11pm; closed Sunday
Credit cards: Interac; Alcohol: no
Wheelchair access: no
*Average main course: $8*

Arirang serves health-conscious home-style Korean cooking on Ste-Catherine Street downtown.

The menu is updated traditional Korean. No MSG is used, and the traditional side dishes served in most Korean restaurants are limited to kimchee. The most popular dish is the bi bim bap, a perfect mélange of beef, chicken, or shrimp with egg and spicy sauce. It is served in a regular bowl or sizzling hot in a stone bowl. Bulgogi is thin strips of tender beef served with crisp vegetables on a hot iron plate (it isn't cooked at the table here). Creamy tofu with seafood is made with a special organic tofu that is feathery light. The dish arrives bubbling hot in a heavy stone bowl, with a poached egg and morsels of seafood in a full-flavoured broth, and served with rice—really delicious. Light, crisp beef dumpling appetizers are served with cold crisp lettuce in a good vinaigrette. Winter specials are hot soups, and summer specials include cold skate (fiery hot), cold noodle soup, and a refreshing red bean dessert.

Peter Park came here with his wife Madam Lee in 2004 and they opened Arirang soon after. He is an engineer and she is a classical Korean singer and member of a Korean church choir. "Arirang" is traditional Korean music—and Madame Lee occasionally sings in the restaurant. They are very health-conscious and want their offerings to reflect what they think is best about Korean food. The space is simply but tastefully decorated. It's comfortable without being luxurious, with tile-topped tables and comfortable chairs. There are stylish stainless steel chopsticks and rice bowls, pottery serving dishes and plates. This is good Korean food without pretence.

# Arzou Express

**6254 Côte-des-Neiges** (corner Van Horne)
Métro: Côte-des-Neiges, then bus 161, 165, or 535
Phone: 514.731.2184
Hours: Sun-Wed 10am-10pm; Thurs-Sat 10am-11pm
Credit cards: V, Interac; Alcohol: beer only
Wheelchair access: no
*Average main course: $8.50; family dinner for 4: $40*

Arzou Express is the only Uyghur restaurant in Montreal, and possibly in Canada.

All the food served here is Uyghur home-style cooking. Excellent grilled brochettes (small and large) are served with salad and rice (avoid the frozen fries). The hand-made *soman* noodles are combined with chopped beef and a lightly piquant sauce—sumptuous comfort food Uyghur-style. One of the star attractions is the *gosh nan*, a generous 8-inch flaky pastry turnover, folded into a half circle, and filled with mildly spiced chopped beef and onions. Pilaf with marinated lamb shank and vegetables is a good choice. The wonton-style soup is in a flavourful beef broth with large homemade dumplings garnished with coriander, onion, and peppers. *Samsa* are savoury meat-filled baked triangles. The cabbage salad is a winner. Dessert includes a sweet noodle square and a puff pastry ball filled with very sweet yogurt filling. A special tea with sugar is a good accompaniment.

Three Uyghur immigrant families opened Arzou Express in April 2005. Uyghur is a Muslim area, bordered by Mongolia, Tibet, and Kazakhstan in the westernmost part of northern China on the old Silk Road. Uyghurs have their own language and are one of the larger minorities in China. The region includes cold rugged mountains, desert steppes and verdant valleys, and the cooking reflects these influences. The decoration is minimalist but the space is pleasant, bright, and extremely clean. There are tablecloths and it feels homey and friendly. Kids are very welcome. You may have to point and gesture to order your food but come to Arzou Express to discover unfamiliar dishes and a warm Uyghur welcome in the tradition of the Silk Road.

# Aux Vivres

**4631 St-Laurent** (near Mont-Royal)
Métro: Mont-Royal, then 97 bus; or 55 bus
Phone: 514.842.3479
Hours: Tues-Sun:11am-11pm; closed Monday
Credit cards: cash only; Alcohol: no
Wheelchair access: no
*Average main course: $7*

Aux Vivres is an alternative vegan resto in the Plateau.

Everything is vegan, virtually everything is made in-house, and many products are organic (from a local organic farm in season), local, or bioethically grown. The menu is international. The sandwiches are very popular with a variety of chapatti sandwiches with fillings such as chickpea curry, BLT (in this case made with smoked coconut, tomato, and sprouts), hummous and tabouleh, and the Vietnamese sandwich made with gingered tofu, marinated daikon, coriander, lettuce, and sprouts. The house specialties are the kitchen's own very successful végépaté and the amazingly good végélox—a delicious maritime-inspired concoction that includes carrots, dulse, onion, and lemon. Delicious tofu cream is a smooth and sweet mixture with the texture of whipped cream, and it's featured in several dishes. The cold plate offers a good variety, and the dragon bowl is also a favourite with brown rice, sprouts, carrots, dulse, and a special dragon sauce. The lunch or evening special is usually an excellent choice, including soup, main plate, a chapatti, a delicious dark chocolate mint truffle, and a tisane.

Aux Vivres started out as a collective begun by Marie Pierre Michaud on Duluth, then Saint-Dominique and finally here where they are comfortably ensconced with folksy mismatched furniture, a nice outdoor terrace, and very special wall treatment in the bathroom. Michael Makhan has been sole owner since 2004 and he's planning to expand in winter 2005. It's a friendly and relaxed place where you can see the food being prepared. But make no mistake, this kitchen may do things in a healthy and ethically responsible way but they are clearly committed to GOOD vegan food!

# B&M

**6200 Somerled** (corner Grand Boulevard)
Métro: Villa Maria, then 103 or 162 bus
**5800 Sherbrooke** (corner Melrose) for takeout and delivery
Métro: Vendôme, then 105 bus
Phone: Somerled: 514.488.1555; Sherbrooke: 514.484.3717
Hours: Mon-Fri 7am-2am; Sat & Sun 9am-2am
Credit cards: V, MC, Amex, Interac (not for delivery);
Alcohol: all (Somerled only)
Wheelchair access: yes
*Average main course: $10*

B&M is an NDG hot spot with a vast menu, large portions, and good food.

It's a challenge to choose from rotisserie chicken, brochettes, steaks, seafood, Chinese dishes, pizza, pasta, salads, sandwiches, and who knows what all! B&M pulls it all off because everything is fresh and made to order. Pizzas are particularly popular, with an excellent thick or thin crust, and myriad toppings and sizes. Pastas include cannelloni, spaghetti, linguini, and fettuccine with standard or "au gratin" versions. Chicken, beef, vegetarian, fish, or combo brochettes are tasty. Salads are large and fresh, with olive oil dressings. There are plenty of vegetarian options. Daily blackboard specials ($8.25-$20) include soup and coffee. Roast beef is available most days and it's a real winner although a little over the Cheap Thrills limit. The usual breakfast/brunch specialties are reasonably priced. Portions are super-generous.

B&M stands for Bob and Mike, long-gone owners of the original place on Monkland at Royal. It was bought in 1983 by Jimmy and Anastasia Farazis, and Kathy, Jimmy, and Chris Soulingis. They turned a greasy spoon into a beloved NDG landmark, popular and welcoming to all generations and especially popular in the West End for thick crust pizza. They moved to nearby Somerled in 2003 and now have a delivery and takeout place on Sherbrooke as well. You could eat here every day without getting bored. It's busy on weekends but there's always a cheerful good feeling about the place. B&M works because it's pleasant, it has lots of variety, portions are big, and the food is fresh and reliably good.

# Ban Lao Thai

**930 Décarie** (near Côte-Vertu)
Métro: Côte-Vertu
Phone: 514.747.4805
Hours: Mon-Wed 11am-8pm; Thurs-Sat 11am-9pm; Sunday
closed; closed two weeks in summer and around Christmas
Credit cards: cash only; Alcohol: BYOB
Wheelchair access: entrance, yes; restroom no
*Average main course: $6.50; combos $14.50*

Ban Lao Thai brings us authentic Laotian fare on the Décarie/
Côte Vertu food strip.

This place is hopping at lunch but it's more relaxed in the
evening. The combos are a wonderful way to discover authentic
Laotian specialties, including a complex and funky green
papaya salad, an addictive treat that's available Laos-style with
crab paste or the more familiar Thai-style with shrimp paste.
But the best thing in the house is the splendid plump Laotian
sausages made by Outtama Phonsavanh, the owner's mother—
they are worth a trip across town! They are a perfectly-textured
mixture of ground pork, lemongrass, lime leaves, garlic,
cilantro, a touch of hot pepper, and who knows what other
secret ingredients. Sausages are served beautifully browned
with lettuce and cool, crisp bamboo shoots. This is NOT La
Belle Fermière territory! Sticky rice is a must, served in
charming little baskets with plastic liners that keep the rice
piping hot. Laotian food can get very, very hot so indicate your
preferred level of chilies very carefully.

The Silavong family worked in the food business when they
came here from Laos, opening the Laotian grocery store next
to the restaurant in 1989. They sold the store in November
1999 to concentrate on the restaurant. It's a family affair with
mother in the kitchen and dad and daughter Diana pitching
in. It's a pleasant but unassuming place and the sidewalk terrace
out front is great for people watching in good weather. This is
*real* Southeast Asian cooking, not ersatz versions of generic
North American-Oriental. The Silavongs bring us a touch of
home cooking from a very special corner of the world.

# Bangkok

**1616 Ste-Catherine W.** (Le Faubourg at Guy, 3rd floor);
**1639 Ste-Catherine W.**
Métro: Guy-Concordia, or 15 bus
Phone: 514.935.2178; 514.846.1003
Hours: 11am-8:50pm daily; 11:45am-11pm daily
Credit cards: cash only; V, MC, Amex, Interac;
Alcohol: no at 1616; all at 1639
Wheelchair access: yes at 1616; restroom, yes at 1639
*Average main course*: $6.50

Bangkok serves really fine Thai food at affordable prices in a downtown food mall—or in their more peaceful offshoot across the street!

Both Bangkoks have exceptionally good Thai food. The chicken soup is an outstanding light meal, with chunks of chicken (optional coconut milk) and the tart bite of lemongrass—arguably the best chicken soup in town. Set specials are under $7 and include soup or crispy house-made spring rolls and choices like chicken with yellow curry (particularly yummy), cashews or chili paste, and ginger beef. A la carte dishes like pad Thai, garlic and pepper, peanut sauce, and eggplant are available with chicken, beef, seafood or vegetarian options. No pork is served. Eggplant with chicken is sublime, perfumed with Thai sacred basil. Traditional pad Thai is superb in any variation, but the chicken is exquisite. Choose your preferred level of spice or none at all.

Food is made to order (except curries) so everything is fresh with all the complex flavours and textures of Thai cuisine. Chef-owner Somphop Vichenker came here in the 1980s from Bangkok. She rarely leaves the burners in Le Faubourg where she creates her special magic; husband Santisuk and accountant son Phat help manage the business. They've just expanded to be more efficient. Daughter Patty opened across the street in 2004 and her menu and prices are the same but with added specialties such as perfectly cooked whole fried fish. The Faubourg can be noisy and crowded but it's pleasant in the evening; or opt for the quiet charm of Bangkok across the street! Don't miss either one—they're too good to be true!

# Banquise, La

**994 Rachel E.** (at Parc-Lafontaine)
Métro: Sherbrooke or Mont-Royal; or 29 bus
Phone: 514.525.2415
Hours: open 24 hours, closed Christmas Day
Credit cards: Interac; Alcohol: beer only
Wheelchair access: no
*Poutine: $4.40-$10; daily special: $8*

La Banquise serves poutine and diner-style classics 24 hours a day right at the edge of Parc Lafontaine.

They currently have 22 versions of poutine, 44 if you take into account that you can have a regular or large. There's the classic, of course, the Mexican (hot peppers, tomatoes, black olives), Dan Dan (pepperoni, bacon, fried onions), Frank (merguez), T-Rex (ground meat, pepperoni, bacon, smoked sausage), the Elvis (ground meat, peppers, mushrooms) and all manner of other combinations—fries and curd cheese with "everything but the kitchen sink". They also serve club, western, grilled cheese, and BLT sandwiches, spaghetti, shepherd's pie, basic burgers, and Hygrade hotdogs. For an additional $2 you can add soup, dessert and beverage to any main dish. You can also switch your fries to classic poutine for $2.25. There's a daily special that includes dishes like meat loaf or lasagne. The fries are made from fresh potatoes, not frozen, and fried in lard— yes lard—that is changed frequently so the fries never taste stale. Microbrewery beer is available.

There's a crew of young staff (with fairly high turnover) that keeps this place going 24 hours a day, so service can be spotty—sometimes it's friendly, sometimes not. This classic neighbourhood joint, across from a police station and the park, has been going since 1962 but Marc Latendresse and the original owner's daughter, Annie Barsalou, have owned it since 1994. There are cute painted tables and a small charming terrace out back. La Banquise is a great late-night or early morning pit stop for your favourite junk food—but don't check your cholesterol levels right after eating here!

# Barroso Grill

**1480 Ontario E.** (bet. Plessis and Alexandre de Sève)
Métro: Berri-UQAM, then bus 125
Phone: 514.521.2221
Hours: 11am-11pm
Credit cards: Interac; Alcohol: all
Wheelchair access: yes
*Average main course: $10*

Barroso on Ontario East offers superb Portuguese grill at great value in a very charming setting!

The grill staff know their stuff. The menu is all charcoal grill and they do it perfectly. The meat or fish is unfailingly moist and delicious, never undercooked or overcooked. They have pork, quail, lamb chops, a mixed grill (your choice), meaty spare ribs, chouriço, fresh fish, and of course traditional Portuguese grilled sardines. Grilled squid or shrimp are cooked to a delicious crispy perfection. Everything is served with a fresh salad and real fries, not frozen. A sandwich of grilled pork, sausage or chicken is a real deal for less than $7. If you insist on resisting the grilled delights there are salads (tuna, chicken, Caesar). Whole grilled chickens and family packs are available for takeout. It all goes down well with a jug of house wine or a bottle of light and bubbly Sumol. Barroso's espresso machine is a delight to behold and coffee is taken seriously. For dessert try the traditional Portuguese *pastéis de nata*, light custard tart.

Owners Teresa, Sylvestre, and Manuel Barrosa set up this place beautifully and carefully when they opened in June 2003. It has a modern, uncluttered look with sage-coloured walls. It's convivial and efficient and the menu is designed for the budget-conscious. The Barrosa family has owned the more expensive Porto across the street for the past nine years, and they know their business. There may soon be a second Barroso in the West End. Great grill food, great value, for a crowd or an intimate rendezvous.

# Beniamino & Co.

**32 McGill** (near de la Commune)
Métro: Square Victoria, or 61 bus
Phone: 514.284.1711
Hours: Mon-Fri 8am-10pm; Sat & Sun 9am-9pm
Credit cards: V, MC, Interac; Alcohol: grocery licence for wine
   & beer
Wheelchair access: entrance, yes; restroom, no
*Average main course: $10*

Beniamino is a specialty Italian grocery store on the western edge of Old Montreal—and it also serves delicious take-out food and has seats for eating in.

The menu is mainly Italian specialties and there is always quite a variety, including vegetarian dishes. Portions are generous. Veal meatloaf is excellent, as is the chicken with prosciutto and brie. The lasagna is to die for. Their osso bucco is tender and tasty, napped with a simply perfect tomato sauce. The roast pork tenderloin and General Tao chicken are delicious. There are vegetarian dishes available too. Bruschetta is made with quality ingredients. They have fresh fruit in containers, cannoli, cakes, muffins, pie, and Segafredo coffee.

Beniamino Bello (from Calabria) and Carlo Fiorino (from Campobasso) opened their place in April 2004. They worked in fast food and at Boccocino's for many years before they went on their own. This is really a spiffy Italian specialty food store with a seriously good food counter and facilities for eating in. They also cater. It's a great combo that seems particularly tuned to our current food needs: They sell high-end Italian foodstuffs and gift items, they have a great prepared food counter, and if you want to eat in there are tables at the back among the specialty olive oils or upstairs surrounded by the gift goods. An added bonus is the dry cleaner depot where you can drop off and pick up your cleaning after hours. This is a convenient food stop for eat-in or take-out, and they're open late during week nights!

# Binerie Mont-Royal, La

**367 Mont-Royal E.** (at St-Denis)
Métro: Mont-Royal
Phone: 514.285.9078
Hours: Mon-Fri 6am-8pm; Sat & Sun 7:30am-3pm
Credit cards: cash only; Alcohol: no
Wheelchair access: no
*Daily specials*: $5.99

La Binerie is a classic 1940s working-class diner on the Plateau
Mont-Royal, serving simple food and Québécois specialties.

The day starts with an early-morning trucker-style breakfast
featuring various combinations of eggs, bacon, sausage, toast,
crétons, and baked beans. The house specialty, available any
time, is their homemade baked beans served with bread, and
optional sausages. A complete three-course lunch or dinner
includes pea soup, dessert, and beverage. Main course choices
include typical diner-style specialties like macaroni with meat,
beef with cabbage, sausages, shepherd's pie, and home-grown
Québécois specialties like tourtière, ragoût de boulettes, and
crétons. The House Special ("Assiette Maison") is a combo of
tourtière, ragoût de boulettes, and baked beans—all the
specialties of the house rolled into one extravaganza—and at
$8.95 this is the most expensive item on the menu. Dessert is
the Binerie's famous pudding chômeur, or bread pudding.
Everything is made on the premises from closely guarded
recipes that yield old-timey comfort foods, Québécois-style.
It's impossible to leave here hungry but don't even try to count
the carbs!

There are absolutely no frills in this small friendly place—a
family-run business with only 11 stools and 4 tables. Started
in 1940, it has stayed in the family and both food and surroundings are very much like they have always been. La Binerie takes
us back in time.

# Bistro San Lucas

**2556 Centre Street** (at Charlevoix)
Métro: Charlevoix
Phone: 514.934.3282
Hours: Tues-Sat 5pm-1am; closed Sunday and Monday
Credit cards: V, MC, Interac; Alcohol: all
Wheelchair access: no
*Average daily special: $13 (prices include tax)*

Bistro San Lucas serves home-style Greek cooking in Pointe-St-Charles.

The menu is evolving at this new bistro but for now they have six affordable rotating items every day. (They will expand as they go along.) Everything comes with a huge portion of Greek salad with feta cheese, and wonderful chunky home-fried potatoes. The roster almost always includes crispy (and not rubbery) fried calamari and a hamburger. Other choices might be charcoal grilled lamb chops or steak, veal in tomato sauce, pasticcio (veal with cinnamon, cloves, cheese, and béchamel sauce), moussaka made in heaven, vegetarian items like spinach with tomato sauce, and a jumble of beans, potatoes, zucchini, lemon, and fresh dill. Quality olive oil is used with a deft touch and the food is not floating in it. Many dishes are touched with lemon.

Chefs Nina Simatos and son John bought this former French restaurant in April 2005. Nina's grandfather came here from Greece and for decades the family had a South Shore restaurant (Simatos) where she grew up. Her mother was from the island of Kefalonia in the Ionian Sea so the cooking here is grounded in the Greek Islands, but with one foot in North America. It's a modest space with a bar where locals gather late into the evening. A large oval table with a comfy banquette is at the front window—a great spot for a friendly gathering of friends or family. There are also small tables for two or four and comfortable bistro chairs. A gas fireplace in the back room is cosy in winter, and the large secluded terrace is popular in summer. This is affordable classic Greek island cooking done very well.

# Boîte à Lunch

**6707 Sherbrooke W.** (near Park Row East)
Métro: Vendôme, then 105 bus
Phone: 514.482.0606
Hours: 11am-10pm
Credit cards: V, MC, Interac; Alcohol: no
Wheelchair access: no
*Average main course: $7; table d'hôte: $7.95 (prices include tax)*

Boîte à Lunch is a small place opposite Trenholme Park in NDG offering Romanian/Eastern European specialities and—twenty flavours of ice cream.

The menu includes soups as a first or a main course. The chicken breast schnitzel is the house specialty and it is superb— a generous portion of thin, lightly breaded, moist and tasty cutlets, served with mashed potatoes and a fresh salad, or alternately in a delicious sandwich with Swiss cheese. There are European sausages, stuffed vine leaves, stuffed cabbage leaves served with your choice of yogurt or sour cream, stuffed green peppers, a delightful vegetarian mushroom stew with tomato sauce, and homemade meatballs available in a few incarnations. There are Greek and Balkan salads with feta, and a variety of sandwiches. They use only the freshest produce and everything is made on the premises. This used to be McDoherty's Ice Cream Parlour and the new owners have maintained twenty flavours of ice cream, and ice cream treats such as banana splits, sundaes, milk shakes, and profiteroles. They also serve delicious house apple or cheese strudel, not too sweet. The owner/chefs are very accommodating to special requests, and they also do takeout and delivery.

This is a small and homey place, comfortable and very in-formal. There is a wonderful shaded sidewalk terrace across from Trenholme Park. Taxes are included in the very reasonable prices. The owners (both engineers) came from Romania in 2002 and they opened the restaurant in 2003. Boîte à Lunch serves simple good food with an Eastern European accent, plus some very North American ice cream treats.

# Bombay Choupati

**5011 Sources Blvd.** (near Gouin Blvd, Pierrefonds)
Phone: 514.421.3130
Hours: Tue-Fri 11am-2pm, 5-10pm; Sat & Sun: noon-10pm
Credit cards: V, MC; Alcohol: all
Wheelchair access: no
*Average main course: $8*

Bombay Choupati is a small hidden treasure serving excellent Indian food in a West Island strip mall.

Both vegetarian and meat dishes are on offer. One of the house specialties is the hard-to-find South Indian masala dosa, a light, crisp thin pancake (made here from scratch) filled with curried potatoes and served with a tasty sambal and coconut chutney. Delicious fruit chaat pairs wafers (fried and puffed puri) with potatoes, chickpeas, yogurt, chutney, tomatoes and cucumber, wonderful as an appetizer or combined with other dishes for a meal. Shrimp, goat, or chicken vindaloo are available as are tandoori chicken and curried goat. Butter chicken has a beautiful creamy curry sauce, a far cry from the banal versions that seem to be available in many other places. They serve a variety of thali combo specials that feature pilaf rice and nan bread. Desserts include kulfi (homemade frozen treat made with reduced milk, saffron, cardamom, and pistachio), a good version of the ubiquitous gulab jamun (milk balls in rose-flavoured syrup), or mango ice cream.

Rajani Singnurkar decided to open Bombay Choupati in 1992 after the company her husband Vasant worked for went out of business. They came from India in the 1970s but they haven't forgotten their culinary roots. They both cook and serve in this small but comfortable place (40 seats) decorated simply with a panoply of Indian deities. Everything is made to order, so service can be slow on weekends when they are very busy; weekday service is faster. They only reserve for up to six people. Bombay Choupati serves terrific Indian food on the West Island!

# Bombay Mahal

1001 Jean-Talon W. (at Birnam)
1242 Crescent (at Ste-Catherine W.)
Métro: L'Acadie; Guy-Concordia
Phone: 514.273.3331; 514.392.3888
Hours: Jean-Talon: Tue-Sat 11am-10:30pm; Sun 11am-9pm;
  closed Monday / Crescent: Mon-Fri 11:30 am-3pm,
  5pm-10 pm; Sat-Sun 5pm-10pm
Credit cards: Jean-Talon: cash only /Crescent: MC, Amex, Interac
Alcohol: no / all
Wheelchair access: no
*Jean-Talon average main course: $7;*
*Crescent: lunch buffet $8.95, thali $13*

The original Bombay Mahal on Jean-Talon West and the downtown branch both serve outstanding Gujarati-style food.

Both strictly vegetarian and meat dishes are available. Cooking is Gujarat style with some South Indian specialties. They make sublime masala dosa, with their own batter of fermented rice and dal (lentils)—long, toasty, thin, and lacy handfuls, rolled around a delicious filling and served with sambal and chutney. Tandoor choices include chicken, goat, and shrimp, or a combo dish. Tandoor chicken leg (drumstick and thigh) with salad has to be one of the best buys in town at $2.50! Black lentils with spices are a special treat. Chicken, lamb, and goat dishes are saturated with flavour and spicy goodness. Thalis are a good way to taste a variety of things and they're available until 9 p.m. Onion badji is outstanding with a tamarind sauce, and excellent nan and roti are fresh from the tandoor oven. Take-out and catering is a large part of their business. The downtown branch has an excellent lunch buffet ($8.95) or all-you-can-eat dinner ($15.95) from the menu.

Bombay Mahal ("mahal" means "palace") opened in 1998. The original owner was from Bombay but in 2001 it was sold to Ruksmani Bhandari. Both locations are owned by the same family. Cook and manager Prashant Daroo-wala, originally a lawyer in Gujarat, came to Canada in 1991 and from the beginning he has maintained consistent quality and style. There is non-décor at Jean-Talon, but downtown is quite a pleasant space. Food is excellent and prices good in either location!

# Braseiro

**8261 St-Laurent** (near Crémazie))
Métro: Jarry, then 193 bus; or 55 bus
Phone: 514.389.0606
Hours: Sun-Wed 11:30am-9pm; Thurs-Sat 11:30am-10pm
Credit cards: V, MC, Interac; Alcohol: all
Wheelchair access: yes, through the back door
*Average main course: $9*

Braseiro is a Portuguese gem on St-Laurent near Crémazie.

Things start off well as you nibble on your complimentary olive sampler. It's hard to make a choice as you eye platters leaving the grill heaped with delicious, moist, and perfectly cooked fish, meat, or poultry. You can make a meal of a couple of appetizers or any of the very generous main courses. It can be hard to choose between grilled octopus or grilled squid, both tender, with tasty grilled bits, and beautifully plated with creamy white beans, crisp lettuce with decent dressing, and fresh lemon. Grilled chicken is the house favourite, but the pork and filet mignon are also excellent. A mixed grill can be a good compromise. Everything is grilled perfectly here and the ribs are delicious without being coated with a sweet gooey mess. The fries are fresh, not frozen and cooked fresh in vegetable oil—they're worth straying from virtue. Brasseiro has good desserts but you might not make it. Doggie bags are almost a must. They offer Portuguese specialties at lunch. Everything is cooked to order. Call ahead if you want to do takeout—especially the exquisite whole Frango Chicken ($11).

Gilberto and Joanna Soares came to Montreal from Portugal more than 35 years ago and they previously owned Brasa. In December 2002 sons Dedy and Elvis (he's the accomplished grillmaster) opened Braseiro. It's a friendly relaxed place where you instantly feel at home and ready to dig in, fingers and all. It's simply decorated with glass topped tables with tablecloths, and comfortable chairs. Everything runs smoothly and regulars keep on coming to enjoy great grill food in amiable surroundings.

# Buffet Palace Oriental

**7165 Newman Blvd.** (LaSalle, west of Carrefour Angrignon)
Métro: Angrignon, then 106 bus
Phone: 514.364.6688
Hours: 11am-3pm; 4:30pm-10pm
Credit cards: V, MC, Amex, Interac; Alcohol: all
Wheelchair access: yes
*Buffet: $7.49 (weekday lunch) to $14.99 (weekend dinner)*

Buffet Palace Oriental in Ville LaSalle hits the spot if you are looking for an Asian buffet that includes sushi.

There's no doubt this buffet aims to please all tastes—it has a little bit of everything. The food is rather predictable but there are no unpleasant surprises—it's a good spread with lots of variety, the food is well-prepared, and dishes are fresh since it is replenished regularly to meet the high volume. The best bets are the hot and sour soup, Chinese dumplings, and seafood specialties like Szechuan shrimp and crab legs. If you're not in the mood for Oriental food you can try the chicken wings or the roast beef. The Szechuan mixed veggies are tasty and not overcooked. Fresh fruit and other buffet-style desserts are available. The special treat is that this buffet includes a modest selection of sushi, including various maki rolls and salmon sushi.

Buffet Palace Oriental opened in Ville LaSalle in December 2002. They recently opened a branch in Greenfield Park. It's a family-oriented place but it works well for groups as well. It's kid-friendly, relaxed, open, and bright, although it can be quite noisy when it's crowded. They do delivery and take-out from a special take-out menu that includes a wide selection of dishes. This is a good buffet—and the sushi is a special extra!

# Cabane, La

**3872 St-Laurent** (at Napoléon)
Bus: 55 (St-Laurent)
Phone: 514.843.7283
Hours: 11:30am-3am daily; kitchen closes at 2am
Credit cards: V, MC, Amex, Interac; Alcohol: all
Wheelchair access: yes
*Daily specials: $8-$14*

La Cabane is a resto-bar serving appetizing food at all hours in a convivial spot on St-Laurent Boulevard.

The chalkboards announce the daily specials (including veggies, fries/rice, and coffee) and they usually include a pasta dish, fresh fish (e.g., salmon steak), a game dish (Thursday-Sunday), and a combo plate such as lamb chops/quail/sausage. They're a good deal. Many dishes are charcoal-grilled Portuguese style. Brochettes are popular and the fries are superb—fresh potatoes cooked properly in vegetable shortening! Light and crusty Portuguese rolls are excellent and they make wonderful sandwiches (grilled pork is a favourite). Portions are generous. Petisco is a hefty appetizer or main meal of grilled pork and sausages with cheese—it sounds unlikely but it's wonderfully addictive! The 14-ounce rib steak is a $15 glutton feast! Meat and fish lovers will be very happy here but vegetarians will find comfort with the Greek salad. Draft beer in pitchers (including local microbrews) is the accompaniment of choice. If you can manage it, treat yourself to a glass of fine port or, in season, pop next door for a Ripples ice cream.

It's friendly, casual, and comfortable with a youngish crowd. Front windows open up in good weather. The kitchen closes at 2:00 a.m. so you can have a late meal here. Abilio Carrera bought La Cabane in 1980. He died in 2000 but sons Martinho and Eugenio and Derek Melo keep everything running smoothly, adding new touches and updates. La Cabane is an ideal place to while away a pleasant afternoon, evening, or late night with a satisfying meal and a pitcher of draft beer.

# Café International

**6714 St-Laurent** (near St-Zotique)
Métro: Beaubien, then 18 bus; or 55 bus (St-Laurent)
Phone: 514.495.0067
Hours: 7am-3am daily; kitchen closes at midnight
Credit Cards: V, MC, Amex, Interac; Alcohol: all
Wheelchair access: entrance (one step); restroom no
*Average daily special: $14*

This authentic café in Little Italy serves great food, excellent coffee and it offers just the right atmosphere!

Bocconcini and tomato, and calamari fritti or grilled appetizers are terrific for grazing. Panini include tuna, chicken, prosciutto, and grilled house sausage. Pizzas are justly popular. Daily specials include pastas, meat, fish, and always a risotto. The kitchen prepares fresh pasta every day, ricotta cavatelli is a specialty. Food is fresh and good. Salads are impeccably fresh! Coffee is the specialty of the house and it's freshly ground and expertly prepared using an extraordinarily fine house blend. The kitchen is now open until midnight.

Café International (opened 1968) was bought in 2001 by Edmondo Arcaro. Son Marco (Cordon Bleu-Ottawa) is the chef and son Michael is the manager. Unlike other coffee bars in the area, food is now front and centre, not an afterthought. You can stand for a quick coffee at the long counter, European-style, but tables and chairs are also available for eating and idling. Front windows slide open in summer. A big TV screen documents the sports scene for those interested. You could spend the whole day here, beginning with coffee and a newspaper in the morning, later meeting with family, friends, or lovers. Young and old, strangers and regulars, all feel comfortable here, enjoying the atmosphere, wonderful food, and the fabulous coffee. One of the great pleasures of a Montreal summer evening is sitting at crowded outside tables late into the night, eating, sipping, viewing, and being part of the vibrant passing street scene of Little Italy. Café International is a convivial Italian-style café!

# Café L'Étranger

**680 Ste-Catherine W.** (near Université)
Métro: McGill
Phone: 514.392.9016
Hours: Mon-Wed 9am-11pm; Thurs & Fri until 12am; Sat 11am-
    12am; Sun 11am-11pm
Credit cards: V, MC, Interac; Alcohol: all
Wheelchair access: no
*Specials of the day: $9-$10*

Café L'Étranger serves a wide selection of comfort food in a
relaxed spot, a few steps down, in the heart of downtown.

The sheer abundance of the menu is overwhelming: salads,
snacks, sandwiches, burgers, pizza, panini, and wraps. The daily
menu (11am-11pm) changes weekly and it includes breakfast,
a burger, panini, Caesar salad, a pasta, and a few substantial
dishes like chicken pot pie or sweet and sour meatballs. Snack/
appetizer Hunan dumplings (great sauce) are very popular.
Salads are fresh and tossed with a variety of good dressings.
The menu has 13 varieties of grilled cheese sandwich—a stag-
gering but deliciously interesting array, served with the signature
crunchy pasta chips. Sandwiches and burgers come in
interesting combinations with grilled veggies and other goodies.
Ice cream desserts are huge extravaganzas that could be shared
by a group. The candy bar fiesta is utterly decadent! The bar
serves novelty mixed drinks and a large selection of imported
beer and local microbrews.

Doreen Tang and Rick Mok opened L'Étranger in 1998, the
name inspired by the Camus novel, and it aims to be a place
where strangers can feel at home, have a drink or a meal, or
settle in to read something from the bookshelves. Kitchen and
wait staff are young, energetic, and they keep things moving.
It's a good place to go for lunch, dinner, or a snack while
shopping, after a movie, or a hard day at the office. This is a
pleasant downtown place with good food and reasonable
prices.

# Café Rococo

**1650 Lincoln** (bet. Guy & St-Mathieu)
Métro: Guy-Concordia
Phone: 514.938.2121
Hours: Tue-Fri 10am-10pm; Sat 11am-10pm;
    closed Sunday & Monday
Credit cards: V, MC, Amex; Alcohol: all
Wheelchair access: no
*Average main course*: $8

Rococo is one of very few Hungarian restaurants in Montreal.
The menu includes many Hungarian favourites. Portions are large, but the leftovers are good too! The plump fragrant cabbage rolls, full of juicy flavour, have a nicely spiced filling of rice and meat. Cabbage noodles and noodles with egg are the stuff of comfort food dreams. Chicken liver with onions and sweet paprika is a big favourite, followed by excellent chicken paprikash or the not-to-be-missed classic goulash. Salad dressing is deliciously sweet and tart. Soups are filling and are like your grandmother always said they should be. They also have the delicious and nutritious Dr. Joe Schwarcz's incredible vegetarian goulash! It's low-cal but filling—a secret recipe with tofu and an unbelievable sauce. Vegetarian mushroom goulash with an egg on top is also a great choice. Maybe the best thing they make is the yummy thin Hungarian pancakes, palacsinta. The dessert palacsinta come with a chocolate sauce with secret ingredients that surely come from another planet. You'll fight over the last drop! The cakes are divine indulgences, all made in-house. This is authentic Hungarian comfort food.

Rococo opened in 1996. The Pragai family arrived from Hungary in 1988. Jyorjyi is the chef, husband Jozses is the pastry chef and son Tamas is out front. It's a pleasant and comfortable place, with an outdoor terrace. They are unfailingly friendly and helpful. Some regulars eat here Tuesday through Saturday; it's varied, economical, and you definitely won't leave hungry. Rococo serves Hungarian home cooking that just makes you feel good!

# Caffe Grazie Mille

**58 Fairmount W.** (corner Clark)
Bus: 55 (St-Laurent); or 80 (du Parc)
Phone: they don't have one
Hours: Mon-Fri 7:30am-6:30pm; weekends 8:30am-6:30pm;
    summer: open until 8:30pm
Credit cards: no; Alcohol: no
Wheelchair access: no
*Average panino: $6, or $10 with salad*

Caffe Grazie Mille is a great drop-in spot on Fairmount for panini and fabulous Illy coffee.

The fresh-and-simple chalkboard menu invites a Tuscan-style quick Italian meal. They serve panini, salads, biscotti, and tiramisu. The panino ingredients include excellent ciabatta bread, prosciutto, salami, turkey, cheese, veggies, tomato, basil, olive oil, mozzarella, provolone, chevre—so it's hard to go wrong with any choice you make. The panini are then grilled just so! Salad is fresh with excellent olive oil dressing, and generous enough to serve two. Continental-style breakfast is toast with cheese, marmalade, and peanut butter or Nutella, and of course the splendid Illy coffee—considered by some to be among the best in the world. It's always a delicious indulgence when you can find it. (They sell it to brew at home too.) They offer an eclectic selection of sparkling water, fruit sodas, and bottled iced teas. They do a good takeout business—these are great panini.

Owner Franco Gattuso is the son of the Calabrian *nonna* Caterina from Piatto della Nonna. On a trip to Tuscany he was inspired to open a place that would provide an affordable full course meal of quality Italian ingredients between two pieces of bread. He opened this snack bar/café in the fall of 2003. Caffe Grazie Mille has all the authentic charm of a friendly Italian neighbourhood quick stop café, complete with counter, metal bar stools, some high round tables, and a small TV where you can catch sports events. The Fairmount sidewalk terrace is a terrific spot for summer dining or dallying. This is genuine Mediterranean comfort food on the run.

# Caraibe Delite

**4816 Ave. du Parc** (near Villeneuve)
Bus: 80 (Parc)
Phone: 514.274.4509
Hours: Mon-Fri 10am-9pm; Sat noon-9pm; Sun 4pm-9pm
Credit cards: no; Alcohol: no
Wheelchair access: entrance, yes; restroom, no
*Roti: $8.50; average main course: $10 (prices include tax.)*

Caraibe Delite serves Guyanese and Caribbean specialties on Park Avenue.

Guyana's history and geography contribute to the rich food traditions of this small northern South American country. It was a Dutch and later a British colony, and black African slaves and indentured Indian labourers were brought in to work the sugar plantations. Despite its location as part of South America, strong ties developed to the Caribbean, and the population is English-speaking, of East Indian, Black, native Indian, and Chinese origin. Rice is a main crop and is an important part of the diet. Curries, roti, seafood, and Creole influences are all part of the cuisine. Everything is made fresh in-house, including Rita's absolutely stupendous hot sauce. It adds special flavour as well as your choice of spice level to anything on the menu. This hot sauce is worth a trip across town—or even further if you must. Roti and curries are fabulous and are available with shrimp, goat, chicken, or tropical fish. The jerk chicken is outstanding, as are the addictive potato balls. Goat chow mein is uniquely Guyanese!

Bo and Rita Singh opened Jardin du Cari in 1997 introducing Rita's dazzling hot sauce to many adoring customers. They left the St-Viateur eatery and headed for Ontario in 2001, but they have recently come back to what they consider "home," opening this new place in February 2005. The space is simple, uncluttered, comfortable. The appetizing smells wafting from the kitchen are all the decoration one needs. Caraibe Delite's cooking is a wonderful blend of all the diverse influences of Guyana. And of course, we can all rejoice that Rita's hot sauce is back in town!

# Caverne, Le

5184A Côte-des-Neiges (near Queen Mary)
Métro: Côte-des-Neiges; or 165 bus
Phone: 514.738.6555
Hours:11am-10pm daily (to midnight Fri-Sat)
Credit cards: Interac; Alcohol: all
Wheelchair access: no
*Average main course: $9*

Le Caverne in Côte-des-Neiges serves splendid authentic Russian food.

Most plates are served with delicious marinated fresh mushrooms, shredded carrots, and beet salad. The lunchtime table d'hôte has 14 combinations of regular menu items. Thick cabbage borscht soup has lots of dill. The house specialty is *Pogrebok*, two large juicy pork chops cooked in a light egg batter, and served with wonderful fried potato cubes. Pelmoni homemade dumplings are slightly larger than tortellini, filled with meat, then boiled and served with a fresh tomato relish and sour cream—juicy, tasty, and addictive! Vareniki dumplings are stuffed with potato, mushrooms, cabbage, cheese, or sour cherries. Dumplings come in small, medium, and large portions. They also have cabbage rolls, chicken Kiev, and meat-stuffed vine leaves, as well as thin blini with meat, veggies, or sweet cherries. There's a honey layer cake for dessert. Meals can be accompanied by refreshing homemade kvass, Russian beer, or small carafes of viscous frozen vodka in portions of 1, 2, 4, 8, 12 shots, ($2.50-$21) or a full litre ($75).

Leonid Likhton bought a pizzeria in 2001 and slowly added Russian food until there was no more pizza. Recent émigrés from Kazakhstan, he's a musician and his wife is a cook, and it's very much a family endeavour. There are small cloth-covered wooden tables that fit together for large or small groups. There's live current Russian music on Friday and Saturday evenings. There are faux and real stone walls and a stuffed bear head to evoke the cavern atmosphere. It can get crowded and somewhat boisterous on weekends as the vodka flows, but it's convivial. Don't miss this irresistibly good Russian food—it's the real thing!

# Chalet Bar B-Q

**5456 Sherbrooke St. W.** (near Girouard)
Métro: Vendôme; or 105 bus
Phone: 514.489.7235
Hours: Sun-Wed 11am-11pm; Thurs until midnight;
    Fri & Sat until 1am
Credit cards: V, MC, Interac; Alcohol: beer & wine
Wheelchair access: entrance yes; restroom no
*Quarter chicken with fries, coleslaw, and BBQ sauce: $6.25-$7.25*
    *at lunch, $7.65-$8.65 after 3 pm*

Chalet Bar B-Q is a Montreal tradition, still going strong in NDG.

They do one thing—rotisserie chicken—and they do it outstandingly well. The quarter chicken lunch special is a great deal. They also serve hot chicken sandwiches and wings. But the overwhelming favourite is beautiful rotisserie chicken cooked to crispy golden perfection with a juicy interior, served with fabulous BBQ sauce for dunking. Fries cooked in vegetable oil are great, but you can have a baked potato if you insist on being virtuous. Depending on your appetite, choose a quarter (leg or breast portion—breast portions are a little extra), a half, or a whole. Predictable but absolutely delicious! The traditional dessert is that 1950s standby, Boston cream pie, but they also serve coconut cream and pecan pie.

These folks have been cheerfully and efficiently welcoming satisfied customers since Marcel Mauron opened Chalet Bar B-Q in 1944. Louise Mauron McConnell (Marcel's daughter) owns it now and David Theiventhiran is the manager. They had a kitchen fire in early 2005, but to everyone's relief they are back with no visible changes. There is knotty pine wood paneling throughout—the cliché Swiss chalet. Booths are comfortable and it's all very relaxed for single diners, couples, and groups. Most of the staff are veterans (Lucia Tuccia has been a waitress since 1952). Service is prompt and friendly, even when they are busy. The place runs like clockwork. They do a booming take-out business and deliver without charge. There are reception rooms upstairs and free parking in the rear. There are many imitators but Chalet Bar B-Q is the Real Thing!

# Chez Badi

**1675 de Maisonneuve W.** (between St-Mathieu and Guy)
Métro: Guy-Concordia; or 15 or 24 bus
Phone: 514.932.6144
Hours: 11am-2am
Credit cards: MC, Interac; Alcohol: all
Wheelchair access: yes, access through adjacent space
*Average main course: couscous or tagine is $13.50*

Chez Badi serves up home-style Moroccan food downtown.

The chalkboard menu here is a celebration of Moroccan cuisine. Harira (chunky chickpea soup) is Moroccan comfort food, and they do it well, as a first course or a satisfying meal by itself. The house pastilla is a seven-inch circle of ultra fresh and crisp pastry leaves holding a divine stuffing of chicken, crunchy nuts with a subtle touch of sugar and cinnamon. It is served with a generous helping of fresh fruit. The lamb couscous is another specialty, a generous lamb shank (the lamb is from the rolling hills of Charlevoix) and vegetables, everything cooked to the exact degree of "doneness," and served with a wonderfuol soup/sauce over the couscous. They also serve merguez, flavourful tagines, fried fish, and typically Moroccan salad side dishes. The mint tea is done as it should be and it is a perfect complement to the food. Homemade donuts with honey are available on Sunday. They also serve breakfast (eggs, sausage, café au lait) and the baguette sandwich with fries and salad is a deal , $10 at lunch or dinner.

The amiable Khadija Badi Moutia came to Canada in the 1980s to study, but he made his home here. He stayed first in Québec City, then Vancouver, working in restos and hotels, finally opening this family business in 1999. There is lots of space, comfortable chairs, a Berber carpet in the centre of the floor, and a breezy sidewalk terrace to while away the evening sipping mint tea. Moroccan news (in Arabic and French) and special sports events (especially soccer) are discreetly available by satellite TV. This is a delicious little corner of Morocco!

# Chez Benny

5071 **Queen Mary** (at Décarie)
Takeout: **2075 St-Louis**, (near Marcel-Laurin) Ville-St-Laurent
Métro: Snowdon
Phone: 514.735.1836
Hours: Sun-Thurs 11am-11pm; Fri 11am-sundown;
    Sat: sundown-3 am
Credit cards: V, MC, Interac Alcohol: beer and wine only
Wheelchair access: yes
*Average main course: $9; $13 for Chinese dishes*

Chez Benny serves a large variety of good quality kosher fast food—and it does it fast and inexpensively.

You can get it all here: grilled chicken, schwarma, merguez, schnitzel, shish taouk (marinated grilled chicken, Israeli-style), chicken brochette, falafel, hamburgers and hotdogs, not to mention sesame beef, lemon chicken, and vegetarian chow mein. It's a glorious carnival of food from around the world! They do a tremendous volume here so the food is fresh and replenished frequently. Fries are fresh cut and fried twice in vegetable oil, and they're really good! It may be predictable but it's all kosher, all good, all the time—no surprises. However, the falafel with toppings is an exquisite messy delight! Schwarma is great! You choose your food as you go through a cafeteria-style line, pay at the cash, and then sit down at a table—or perhaps two or three, since a lot of table-hopping goes on here! You can have most plates with or without the salad bar. There's a busy terrace in front. They also cater and do takeout, although the lineup can be daunting.

Benamin Cohen started out on Chabanel in 1991 serving the textile industry with quality kosher food, served quickly and without fuss, and at reasonable prices. Michael Assedo joined him and they moved to Queen Mary in 1996. They moved to this location in 2003 with the same formula but an expanded menu. It's been a huge success, and it's busy all the time. A new branch opened in Ville-St-Laurent in August 2005 where they plan to concentrate on fast takeout. Chez Benny is sort of a one-stop kosher food fair!

# Chez Bong (Chinatown)

**1021-B St-Laurent** (at Lagauchetière)
Métro: St-Laurent; or 55 bus
Phone: 514.396.7779
Hours: Tues-Sun 11am-9pm; closed Monday
Credit cards: no; Alcohol: all
Wheelchair access: no
*Average main course*: $9

This Chez Bong serves authentic Korean food in Chinatown.

There are many places that claim to serve Korean food, but too often it's Korean-style rather than the real thing. Chez Bong serves the real thing. The emblematic bi bim bap is excellent, a nicely arranged mixture of rice, veggies, egg, and meat cooked to perfection and served in a stone bowl, with a very good dipping sauce. The dumplings are homemade with tell-tale irregular shapes, juicy, crisp, and toothsome. Beef BBQ ribs are tender and succulent, served steaming hot on a super-heated iron dish. The sweet potato noodles are soft with an interesting texture—a nice change. The kimchee is sharp and tasty. The soup has quite a bite but pleasantly so. The typical cold side dishes are delicious and they complement the dishes and the kimchee. Corn tea is unusual, but a pleasant and re-freshing accompaniment or you can try the Chinese beer.

The owner Bong Lim Lee had Korea House on Queen Mary for 15 years. She retired some time ago but got bored so she opened here in 2003, and she's assisted by her daughter Anne.

The space is nicely set up with natural wood tables and paneling, and bistro chairs. Everything is well organized and the place has been set up for efficiency—the hallmark of an experienced restaurateur doing what she loves to do. Chez Bong is a great place to share authentic Korean food with friends or family.

# Chez Bong (Downtown)

1236 Mackay (below Ste-Catherine)
Métro: Guy-Concordia; or 15 bus
Phone: 514.935.8344
Hours: 11am-10pm, closed Sunday
Credit cards: no ; Alcohol: no
Wheelchair access: no
*Average main course: $9*

This new Chez Bong (no relation to the one in Chinatown) serves outstanding Chinese Korean food downtown.

This food is as authentic Korean as you can get in Montreal. They have regular Korean specialties such as bulgogi, galbi, and bi bim bap and they are well cooked, well presented, and very good indeed. But they also have a whole different style of Korean cooking that is really not available anywhere else in Montreal: Chinese Korean food. *Tang su uk* is fried pork in several variations, including sweet and sour that comes with fruit salad and crunchy vegetables. Jajang mein is a mild but delicious signature light noodle dish with black bean sauce and vegetables, pork, or beef. Many other noodle dish variations combine beef, pork, and seafood. *Naing kong gook su* is a refreshing cold soybean soup with noodles and peanut sauce. There are combo plates, and dishes for two at very good value. The food is prepared with a knowing hand and tastes are mild not strong, allowing natural flavours of the ingredients to stand out. This is a menu with many unfamiliar items and it's fun to explore things you haven't tasted before.

Owner Jun Jeongmi and chef husband Lee Ki Seong opened Montreal's second restaurant called Chez Bong in late 2004. This place is on the spacious middle floor of a simply decorated converted Victorian town house with high ceilings, decorative trim, and a fireplace. They speak mainly Korean but the menu is in English and French, and they are friendly and anxious to help. Chez Bong downtown is an adventure in good eating, Chinese Korean-style.

# Chilenita, La

**64 Marie-Anne W.** (at Clark)
Phone: 514.982.9212
Bus: 55 (St-Laurent)
Hours: 10:30am-8pm daily
**152 Napoléon** (at de Bullion)
Phone: 514.286.6075
Bus: 55 (St-Laurent)
Hours: 10am-6pm, closed Sunday
Credit cards: cash only; Alcohol: no
Wheelchair access: no
*Empanadas $2.25 ea; $23.50/doz; average sandwich: $5*

La Chilenita in the Plateau serves tempting empanadas and some Mexican treats.

Some of the best empanadas in Montreal are baked in these two tiny spaces, made by hand daily with the best ingredients and knowing fingers. The dough is perfect—and the pleasing shapes hold the fillings with style and grace. There are thirteen varieties, and six of them are vegetarian. Fillings include chicken, chorizo, sausage, tuna, seafood, and various vegetarian choices. The big winner is the classic beef and onions, accented with black olive and a small piece of hard-boiled egg. It all comes together perfectly, complemented by the homemade salsa. These empanadas make a wonderful snack or a satisfying meal. They serve interesting sandwiches, including a delicious grilled steak with tomato and avocado, and many vegetarian choices. They also have Mexican specialties including great tacos, enchiladas *rojas* (with "red" tomato sauce), quesadillas, and some of the best burritos in town. This food is the real thing, not a fast-food look-alike. There are also good salads. For dessert try house-made *alfajores*, sandwich cookies with a yummy caramel *dulce de leche* filling, topped with coconut.

Both locations are modest and the food is the real draw, but Marie-Anne is larger. Owner Bernarda Lara, a vegetarian, has created the vegetarian fillings. Take-out is a big part of their business, including food for parties. Order 24 hours ahead for large quantities of mini empanadas and burritos. This is such a friendly and unassuming place it's like going to your aunt's house and sitting in her kitchen while she cooks your favourites.

# Chino-Soul

**6490 Victoria** (near Plamondon)
Métro: Plamondon, or bus 124, or 160
Phone: 514.736.2233
Hours: Mon-Wed 10am-2am; Thurs-Sat 10am-3am;
    Sun noon-2am
Credit cards: V, MC, Interac; Alcohol: all
Wheelchair access: no
*Average main course: $8*

Chino-Soul is a restaurant/bar with a pool table and both Jamaican and Asian food.

There are daily specials and the menu is posted on the board. They have all the popular Caribbean dishes. It's all good and authentic Caribbean food made by two Jamaican cooks, and served with rice and peas (beans) and salad. Roti wrappers and patties are brought in. Best bets are the stew beef or chicken, oxtail and goat curries, jerk chicken, and buffalo wings—all really good and made here from scratch. Chino-Soul also has a Thai cook who prepares various Asian specialties Monday through Thursday evenings: noodles, pad Thai, General Tao chicken, fried shrimp on a skewer, and teriyaki chicken. They do a lot of takeout but only deliver locally.

Peter Liburd from Dominica opened Chino-Soul in 2002 and it's become a popular neighbourhood place to eat and to socialize. He started out with a Thai partner, and although he is now sole owner, the Thai cook remains. You can play pool for $1 a game, have a drink, and enjoy Island or Asian cooking at Chino-Soul. The décor is nothing to speak of. The pool table with overhead green lamps dominates the space and it's in almost constant use. Hip-hop music videos or movies may be playing on the large screen and a smaller TV usually features sports. There is a bar with stools for drinking and socializing, plus bistro chairs and small square tables for eating. A couple of tables with chairs are out front in summer. Food is available until closing time. It's hard to beat pool and good eats!

# Chuch

**4088 St-Denis** (at Duluth)
Métro: Sherbrooke
Phone: 514.843.4194
Hours: Sun-Wed 11am-10pm; Thurs-Sat 11am-11pm
Credit cards: V, MC, Amex, Interac; Alcohol: BYOB
Wheelchair access: no
*Small plate: $7, large plate $10*

Chuch serves spectacularly good vegetarian Thai food in chic surroundings on Saint-Denis.

Chuch is a quick stop for wonderful vegetarian Thai food. One orders from the counter selections or if you wish you can order from the more extensive and pricier ChuChai menu. The counter displays appetizing noodles, tofu, and vegetaria,n chicken, or duck dishes that are all made from seitan. The food is extraordinarily delicious, and beautifully prepared with fresh high-quality ingredients—appealing to the eye as well as the palate. It can be quite a challenge to choose from the selections available so you might have to come back—and many do! It's all so good you won't even notice that it's vegetarian—it's just great food! For dessert there is superb tapioca pudding, cheesecake or mousse cake. Takeout is available.

Owners Patrick Michaud and Lily Sirikittikul opened the very successful ChuChai in 1997. In 1999 they launched the budget-minded and more relaxed Chuch. Service at Chuch is efficient, there is a serene atmosphere, dim lighting, stylish décor with gorgeous chairs, and no one rushes you. There is a very popular terrace in front in good weather. The adjacent ChuChai has a more diverse and upscale vegetarian Thai menu and they also serves alcohol. Chuch also does takeout. This is Thai vegetarian cooking brought to a whole other level at painless prices and in a stylish setting to boot—a winning combination!

# Cobalt

312 St-Paul W. (near St-Pierre)
Métro: Square-Victoria, or 61 bus
Phone: 514.842.2960
Hours: 11:30am-3am, closed Tuesday during the winter
Credit cards: V, MC, Amex, Interac; Alcohol: all
Wheelchair access: yes
*Average main course: $12 (prices include tax)*

Cobalt is a friendly neighbourhood eatery and bar on the edges of Old Montreal where there is live jazz on Wednesday and Sunday evening and for Sunday brunch.

The daily chalkboard specials ($14-$18) list inspired combinations such as trout in tequila sauce with spicy black beans. The regular menu is limited but interesting: panini, salads, and assorted appetizers. The roast lamb panino is a winner. The lamb is warm, slightly pink, tender, and lean, dressed with a Provencale-style mustard. Roast pork panino with blue cheese, pears, and walnuts is great. Appetizers include a Québec cheese platter, tapenade, and other good things that could be combined to make a meal. Salads include inspired combinations like shrimps, spinach, pickled ginger, and sesame seeds, or emmental, grilled cashews, and endive. There is Lavazza espresso. Brunch with live jazz is available weekends 11:30 am-4 pm with French toast, eggs en cocotte, blueberry pancakes, and mimosas.

Musician brothers Nick and Dan Philippi (they previously owned Old Montreal dépanneurs) and Nadia and Pauline Leclerc opened the place in 2003. It has become a favourite Old Montreal spot for locals for lunch, dinner, or a late night drink, especially when there is live jazz. Cobalt is an a charming old stone building with cobalt blue walls, wooden floors, a large front window that's open in good weather, exposed ceiling beams, and there are dim lights and candles at night. It's a friendly place where you can comfortably hang out, and one of the owners even occasionally does card tricks at the bar. Good food at reasonable prices, live jazz, and good vibes are hard to find anywhere but especially in Old Montreal!

# Cracovie

**5349 Gatineau** (near Jean-Brillant)
Métro: Côte-des-Neiges; or 165 bus
Phone: 514.731.3388
Hours: Tues-Sat 11:30am-10pm; Sat-Sun 5pm-10pm;
    closed Monday
Credit cards: V, MC, Amex, Interac; Alcohol: all
Wheelchair access: yes
*Daily table d'hôte: $8-$14*

Cracovie now serves hearty Polish fare in Côte-des-Neiges.

This is terrific home-style Polish cooking at its best. Veal or chicken schnitzel are large breaded cutlets served with a fried egg, cabbage, and beet salad—talk about gilding the lily! The large portion (almost a foot long!) of highly smoked Polish sausage is served with choucroute and mashed potatoes, just as it should be. Mushroom soup is a highly-flavoured house specialty—a far cry from Cream of Campbell's. Beef stroganoff is strips of tender beef served with plenty of cream-infused gravy and potato dumplings. The pierogi come with cheese, meat, vegetable or fruit stuffing. It's all delicious and filling comfort food. Hot borscht is made from fresh grated beets, and it's full-bodied, and both sweet and slightly tart, exactly as it should be. The nut cake has a delicious nut cream filling. The cheesecake is Polish-style, without fruit topping, but dense, rich, and very good. The excellent sourdough rye bread is the perfect accompaniment—but resist the temptation to fill up on it so much that you won't eat your meal.

Owner Stanislas Ciesielka came from Poland many years ago and he opened Cracovie on Stanley near Ste-Catherine in 1979. In 2002 he moved to Côte-des-Neiges to escape high rents. He delights in his new neighbourhood where he serves old customers, as well as area residents and local hospital and Université de Montréal crowds. The food is always fresh and the service is efficient. Cracovie offers us generous servings of home-style Eastern European fare at very reasonable prices.

# Cuba

**1799 Amherst** (near Ontario)
Métro: Beaudry
Phone: 514.389.7222
Hours: Tues-Sun noon to midnight; closed Monday
Credit cards: V, MC, Interac; Alcohol: all
Wheelchair access: yes
*Average main course: $9.50*

Cuba is a warm and welcoming place near Maisonneuve Market with great Cuban food at unbelievable prices.

The menu includes all the best of Cuban cooking. Most dishes are served with rice (plain or with black beans), your choice of plantains done three different ways, black beans, yucca, and salad. Their roast pork is a masterpiece—a large portion of juicy, lime-imbued meat that has been roasted to tender perfection. The chicken is juicy and tasty, and they have combination plates and special meals—all delicious. There is a variety of terrific sandwiches, named after some of the popular beaches so many Canadians frequent. Seafood platters are beyond the Cheap Thrills limit but you might want to splurge anyway. There are guava, papaya, and other fruit desserts but it's a stretch to eat dessert with the size of the portions. Of course the whole meal gets off to a great start with a mojito.

Esteban Casanas and his family did all the fine renovations and woodwork themselves before they opened Cuba in February 2004. (He is retired from the Cuban merchant marine.) It's quite spiffy, uncluttered, with subdued colours, painted low ceiling beams, beautiful wood tables, chairs with over-the-top cowhide seats, placemats, and menu covers. It comes together very well as kind of old Cuban hacienda-style. Service is helpful and good. They sell Cuban music CDs and a few instruments on the side, and they have live Cuban music on Friday and Saturday. This is a great substitute for a trip to Cuba—and the food here is better and more authentic than the food most tourists get at Cuban resorts!

# Diogènes

**925 Décarie, Ville St-Laurent** (near Côte-Vertu)
Métro: Côte-Vertu
Phone: 514.747.7251
Hours: 11am-11pm daily
Credit cards: V, MC, Amex, Interac; Alcohol: all
Wheelchair access: no
*Average platter*: $11

Diogènes is a very popular Ville St-Laurent Greek grill on a part of upper Décarie that has virtualy become an international food fair.

Grilled meat and fish are the specialties. Portions are very generous and platters include salad, rice, and potatoes—try the new Greek-style roasted potatoes instead of the frozen fries. The pikilia appetizer platter is ideal for sharing or a complete meal. The daily special is popular, as are souvlaki, chicken souvlaki, and combo plates. Everything is expertly grilled with just the right touch—no leathery, dried out chicken or fish here! Lightly breaded filet of sole is tender and moist as is the chicken or lamb. This is a terrific place to go with a crowd, sharing different appetizers and main dishes. Crisp, fresh salads are ideal sides.

Diogènes has been a St-Laurent institution for 25 years. It's often packed but you don't feel squished and the staff doesn't rush you. It's very kid-friendly and there are lots of families, but it works as a date place too. Diogènes was a witty and amusing Greek biographer of philosophers (including the hedonistic Epicurus) and he might feel at home in this sunny, casual spot with its white walls, and white and blue tablecloths, reminiscent of the Greek islands. Long-time cooks Sam, Tony, and Johnny bought the place in August 2005 and they plan to add grilled veggies and more fish, and will make other improvements, including an outdoor terrace. An old favourite is about to get even better!

# L'Exception

**1200 St-Hubert** (at René-Lévesque)
Métro: Berri-UQAM
Phone: 514.282.1282
Hours: Mon-Fri 11am-9pm; closed Sat and Sunday
Credit cards: V, MC, Interac; Alcohol: wine & beer
Wheelchair access: no
*Average burger: $5*

L'Exception is a fun burger joint with panache near the Berri métro.

The big deal here is simply burgers, but they're quite some burger! They have standard beef, or you can have a variation with buffalo, lamb, veal, or pork. Pick your passion! Burger toppings include dill pickle, tomato, mushrooms, onions, lettuce, mayonnaise, and Dijon mustard. For variety add bacon, chile con carne, mozzarella, blue cheese, goat cheese, smoked gouda, emmenthal, cream cheese, or any two-cheese combo you like, and you can mix and match as well. Burgers are a respectable size, moist, with flavour, and served on a Kaiser bun. Fries are spectacular: hand cut and fried in canola oil, with just a dash of secret spice. They also have salads and a few croque monsieur variations, but the main event is definitely meat on a bun dressed to kill.

Guido Tocci and Andreas Parashevopoulos bought L'Exception in 1998. It opened in 1983 and was a favourite hangout of theirs. They jumped at the opportunity to make it their own, and quickly added to the basic menu. Décor is retro cool, with old Coke memorabilia, Marilyn Monroe pictures, and other 50s and 60s relics. The walls are painted great colours and have notes from customers written with silver markers—it's a fun personal touch. The smoking room is in the back so it's quite separate from the rest of the restaurant. Sit back and have a burger and fries with a Coke, or do an adult variation with wine or beer. Grab a free gumball at the register to top it all off. Good burgers, good choice, and funky fun too!

# Keur Fatou

**66 St-Viateur W.** (at St-Urbain)
Bus: 55 (St-Laurent)
Phone: 514.277.2221
Hours: Mon-Wed 12pm-10pm; Thur-Sun 12pm-11pm;
    closed alternate Sundays
Credit cards: cash only; Alcohol: no
Wheelchair access: entrance, yes; restroom, no
*Average main course*: $11

Keur Fatou serves Senegalese/West African specialties and they sometimes feature storytelling and live music too!

Like much West African cooking, the food here relies heavily on peanuts (the main crop in Senegal), and on starches such as plantain, yams, manioc, rice, and couscous. No pork is served. Simple homey ingredients are expertly handled by knowledgeable and caring hands to create classic Senegalese dishes. There are three choices available daily. Chicken mafé is a beautiful mélange of chicken and root vegetables simmered in peanut sauce and served with rice and plantain. *Thieboudienne* (baked fish) is perfectly spiced and moist, and chicken yassa is a delightful mix of lemon, garlic, onions, and chillies in a rich sauce served over rice. *Poisson kaldo* is a blend of fresh and smoked fish in onion sauce served with rice and plantain. Homemade hot sauce is available on the side and is added to your taste—if you wish, it will take you all the way to incendiary! Fresh fruit or yogurt are ideal desserts, and homemade ginger juice with a bit of a kick is special.

Ndiouga is the owner, waiter, cook, dishwasher, and storyteller, assisted by his wife and friends. After clients are served, he will sometimes play a sabar (traditional Wolof drum) and tell stories. Occasionally school groups come by for storytelling, music, and snacks—lucky them! They've been open since 2000 in this small space with beautiful Senegalese printed cotton tablecloths. It's comfortable and casual. At Keur Fatou you feel like you've stumbled into a neighbourhood place in Dakar, and it's a charming spot where the food is home-cooking good!

# L Corridor

**3655 St-Laurent** (near Ave. des Pins)
Métro: Saint-Laurent, then 55 bus
Phone: 514.350.5320
Hours : Mon-Sat noon-11pm, closed Sunday
Credit cards: V, MC, Amex, Interac; Alcohol: no
Wheelchair access: at entrance, one step; restroom, yes
*Average main course: $10*

Great tropical Caribbean food is tucked in the back of the main floor corridor of a former textile manufacturing building on St-Laurent Boulevard.

All the favourite West Indian specialties are available here. Jerk chicken is moist and tasty but not spicy—top it off with the house hot sauce. It comes with the traditional sides of rice and peas, salad, and fried plantain. Goat curry has generous chunks of tender meat with potatoes and chickpeas in a rich flavour-loaded gravy. The oxtail curry is so popular they often run out. The roti (beef, goat, chicken, vegetarian) are flavourful handfuls and the Jamaican patties are good. BBQ corn is available in season—a great quick street food treat! Homemade ginger beer with almond is unique, and the astringent tamarind juice really quenches your thirst. There is an excellent variety of juices. Dessert is ice cream, sherbet, coconut or banana cake, and occasionally key lime pie.

Owner Genevieve Gould, a fashion designer, had her atelier in the Guarantee Building, formerly one of many textile buildings on St. Lawrence, or the Main (now St-Laurent) in what used to be Montreal's bustling garment district. When the building snack bar went bankrupt in 2001, she decided to open her own place. She's brought new life to the L-shaped main floor hallway space with tropical scenes painted on the walls by artists who work there. There are three tables, two counters with stools, and a friendly down-home feeling. It's a pleasant surprise to find such satisfying Caribbean food in this unique space, recalling the glory days of the Montreal textile industry on one of the city's most storied streets.

# Lin et Lin

**1123 Beaubien E.** (near Christophe-Colomb)
Métro: Beaubien
Phone: 514.270.9939
Hours: Tues-Sun 11:30am-9pm; closed Monday
Credit cards: V, MC, Amex, Interac; Alcohol: BYOB
Wheelchair access: no
*Dumplings: 6 for $5-$7; Special complete dinner: $7.50-$9*

Lin and Lin is a tiny haven for delicious homemade Chinese dumplings.

The menu includes many dishes but what makes Lin et Lin memorable are the dumplings. There are seven choices of filling: shrimp, beef, chicken, salmon, lamb, vegetarian, and the chef's special. Plump and tasty, carefully prepared and very fresh, they are served with a fabulous peanut dipping sauce that is close to the sesame sauce they would use in China. These are some good dumplings! Customers travel from near and far for these delicious little bundles. In general, the food is simple rather than fussy, relying on the natural goodness of the ingredients and the time-honored combinations of Chinese cuisine. Beef with black bean sauce melts in the mouth and the General Tao chicken is very nicely done. The hot and sour soup is spicy, as it should be, and wontons in the wonton soup are exceptional. Cheese wontons are made with sweet and fragrant cheese, scallions, and pollock. Lunch specials and dinner specials are very good deals. They do a great deal of takeout, including loads of frozen dumplings for folks to cook up at home.

Nan Zheng Lao (he has studied architecture) and Lin Wang (she was a medical doctor in China) opened Lin et Lin in 2003. It's clean but rather plain, with white walls and plain tables with comfortable cushioned seats. It's functional rather than beautiful. The kitchen is really part of the restaurant, partially screened off by a five foot wall, so it's all very intimate and friendly as he cooks and she serves the food. It may not be luxurious but those delectable dumplings will bring you back again and again!

# Lobby Bar

24 Ave. des Pins E. (near St-Laurent)
Métro: St-Laurent or Sherbrooke; or 55 bus
Phone: 514.844.2112
Hours: Mon-Wed 6pm-10pm; Thurs-Sat 6pm-11pm;
  closed Sunday
Web site: www.lobbybar.ca
Credit cards: V, MC, Amex, Interac; Alcohol: all
Wheelchair access: no
*Average tapas: $8*

Lobby serves oriental tapas and a few Laotian dishes in an intimate spot on Avenue des Pins near St-Laurent Boulevard.

All portions are tapas-style, and you will need about two per person for a full meal, less for a light meal. The best way to eat at Lobby is to go in a group and share the dishes. Chicken in green curry is a standout, a generous portion of delicious and beautifully sauced chicken with depth of flavour. The salmon maki in tempura is an interesting deep-fried salmon roll—it may seem improbable but it works! The spicy grilled beef salad is a delicately spiced, well turned out Southeast Asian salad. Excellent red snapper tartare done in Indonesian style is subtly flavoured. There are also great lunch specials from a pared-down menu, and there are soups too.

Ta Phetranphanh is the young Laotian owner. He fled Laos with his family in the 1970s, and after a Thai refugee camp they came to Canada in 1979. He worked as a waiter before coming up with the idea of oriental tapas, and he opened Lobby in 2004. Ta and his mom do the cooking; dad does the dishes, and Ta serves the customers. The small space is nicely furnished and comfortable and the service is attentive and friendly. Southeast Asian tapas may not seem an obvious choice but it's done well here and it's a place to come with friends or family for a lovely meal with lots of variety.

# Lola Rosa

**545 Milton** (near Université)
Métro: McGill; or 24 (Sherbrooke)
Phone: 514.287.9337
Hours: Mon-Fri 11:30am-9pm; Sat-Sun noon-9pm
Credit cards: no; Alcohol: no
Wheelchair access: yes
*Average main course: $9*

Lola Rosa is now serving international vegetarian food not far from McGill University.

This is an approachable vegetarian menu with dishes from Mexico and elsewhere. Nothing is fried and they try to do everything in a health-conscious way. There is always a quiche and a gratin dish available and they change every couple of days. They recently added Turkish bourek to the menu—spinach, feta, pine nuts, and leeks in phyllo—a wonderful choice that the kitchen executes perfectly. The quesadilla is one of the house specialties, lovely and creamy with avocado, mild cheese, and sour cream. The black bean burrito is also a good bet, as are the 4-cheese lasagna and the tofu curry. The hempburger is their own creation, it's big and tasty with lots of toppings. Heaping platters of nachos are a perennial favourite here. Desserts are extraordinarily good, and they are all done in-house rather than with one of the increasingly popular dessert service providers. The humble but delicious apple crumble is not to be missed and key lime pie is luscious. They make mighty fine lemonade and good coffee.

Sebasien Lacroux, Pascal Hourriez, and Eric Biounaes are from France and they bought Lola Rosa in late 2004. They've changed the décor to warm orange and yellow tones and multicultural touches. The front window slides open and the space is bright, the atmosphere relaxed. There are plants and a wide choice of background music. The new owners are experimenting with the menu (handwritten on the wallboard) to introduce more international dishes, but they will remain focused on quality vegetarian food that is interesting and appealing.

# Los Planes Pupuseria

**531 Bélanger E.** (near Châteaubriand)
Métro: Jean-Talon
Phone: 514.277.3678
Hours: 11am-10pm daily
Credit cards: Interac; Alcohol: no
Wheelcair access: no
*Pupusas: $1.85 each; average meat platters: $13*

Los Planes is a typical El Salvador *pupuseria* on Bélanger.

There's a great lunchtime special and they serve a number of huge platters of beef, chicken, or pork with rice and beans, fried yucca, salad, and tortilla. They are all delicious and extremely generous portions, but the real reason to go to Los Planes is for a pupusa feast. The fried pupusas are fresh and not greasy. The bean filling is smooth and creamy. Pile onto the pupusas marinated cabbage, bright red (mild) salsa, and marinated whole jalapeno pepper, then try to restrain yourself from emptying the big jar of marinated quartered onions. These onions are very special. The restaurant imports cane sugar blocks (wrapped in corn leaves) from El Salvador and makes their own marinade by slowly cooking the sugar with white vinegar until the precise moment when the colour and sweet/sour balance are just right. The onions are perfect and they are a knockout with the pupusas. If you dare, add a side order of fried plantain with more frijoles on the side and then dig in. Heaven!

This is a small non-smoking space seating about 45 people at tables with glass-covered tablecloths. Salvadoran artifacts adorn the walls, and Central American popular music plays when satellite television is not beaming in El Salvador programs. The grandmother of owner Gladis Maribel Funes, Paula Funes, is reputed to have developed pupusas in Los Planes de Renderos, a small Salvadoran city that now has 242 *pupuserias*. Gladis is doing her best to bring the *pupuseria* tradition to her new neighbours in the north. Montrealers have taken these delicious treats to their hearts since she opened Los Planes in 1994.

# Ma's Place

**5889 Sherbrooke W.** (at Clifton)
Métro: Vendôme, then 105 bus
Phone: 514.487.7488
Hours: Mon-Wed 11am-9pm; Thurs-Sat until 10pm;
    Sun 11am-8pm
Credit cards: Interac; Alcohol: no
Wheelchair access: no
**850 Décarie** (Ville St-Laurent)
Métro: Côte-Vertu
Phone: 514.744.2011
Hours: Mon-Wed 11am-9pm; Thurs-Sat until 10pm
Credit cards: Interac; Alcohol: all
Wheelchair access: no
*Average meal: small $8, large $12*

Simple and seductive Jamaican cooking is available for eat-in or take-out in the original NDG location and in the Ville Saint-Laurent food strip.

The soup of the day is a meal in itself. It could be chicken, cow foot, or fish soup on Fridays. Mainstay Jamaican specialties like jerk chicken, curried goat, salt fish and ackee, or oxtail stew and roti are the very best kind of home-style cooking. Most dishes are served with traditional rice and beans and plantains. Portions are generous. Tasty homemade hot sauce packs a punch and complements the food beautifully. Ma's patties are considered to be among the best in the city—they're made in-house (not imported from Toronto like many others). They're often sold out. Homemade ginger beer is a satisfying thirst-quencher. They do loads of takeout, especially on Sherbrooke.

The original in NDG is very small but the wall mural makes it seem like you are cutting through the jungle on a sunny, hot day. The new location is much larger and the palm trees and beach scenes on the wall make you feel like you are in Jamaica. Ma (Delma Francis) turned this restaurant over to her son-in-law Eric Blagrove a few years ago. Although he had no restaurant experience he claims to have learned how to cook from his Jamaican mother. Both these moms must have been legendary Jamaican cooks. Eric knows what he's doing, and he ensures the food is good and the atmosphere easygoing.

# Maison du Bedouin

**1616 Ste-Catherine W.** (Le Faubourg at Guy, 3rd floor)
Métro: Guy-Concordia
Phone: 514.935.0236
Hours: 11am-9pm daily
Credit cards: cash only; Alcohol: no
Wheelchair access: yes
*Average main course: $7*

This is an oasis of North African food in a most unlikely setting—a fast food stand in Le Faubourg mall!

The Bedouin's House continues to expand its menu and provide delicious food that's a little different. Daily specials with salad and rice include succulent meatballs in a rich gravy, merguez sandwich, a vegetarian plate chock full of various stewed goodies, and a delectable pastilla with almonds, chicken, and a hint of rosewater. During the colder months harira is available. This life-sustaining chickpea soup traditionally breaks the Ramadan fast. Chicken and veal tagine are tasty Moroccan stews with rich gravy served over saffron rice or couscous. Lamb merguez is mild and savoury. Combo plates allow you to taste more than one thing and they're a good bet. They use halal meat. Turkish coffee is available, but the real winner is the mint tea— made the proper way with fresh mint in a metal pot, and served in charming traditional tiny glass cups. There is a small selection of pastries but the freshly made donuts are irresistible. Ask for some honey on the side to make them even more delectable!

Khalil, the Moroccan owner and chef, has created a small but diverse and authentic North African menu in this compact and well organized food mall stand. They recently moved a few steps away from their original location. This is a great place for lunch when Le Faubourg is busy, but it's also very pleasant in the afternoon or evening when it is quieter. Moroccan mint tea is a great choice any time.

# Maison du Kebab

**820 Atwater** (near St-Antoine)
Métro: Lionel-Groulx
Phone: 514.933.0933; 514.933.7726
Hours: 11:30am-11pm daily
Credit cards: no; Alcohol: no
Wheelchair access: no
*Average main course: $10*

Maison du Kebab is a quick, friendly stop for Persian food on lower Atwater.

Servings are generous and the menu is focused on grilled kebabs served with rice. They use saffron and other Persian spices liberally, and ground sumac is available at every table. Everything is made fresh to order with quality ingredients. A generous side order of colourful parsley, radishes, and raw onions is served with the food. The homemade yogurt is creamy with a tart tang, as real yogurt should be, nothing like the sweetened and gelatinized commercial product we know so well. Appetizers include yogurt with refreshing mint and cucumber, and a delicious dish with eggplant, tomatoes, and onions—simple but very good. Shish kebab brochettes, chicken, or filet mignon kebabs are grilled just so and served with rice. There are various combination meals available—and they're so generous that almost everyone leaves with a doggie bag! Dessert is superfluous but the delicious saffron ice cream made in-house has a delicate flowery taste and vibrant saffron colour. Call ahead for takeout to avoid a long wait.

Farzad Molay has been in the food business here for more than 20 years (he had Khayam on Ste-Catherine) and he and his son now run Maison du Kebab. It's relaxed, friendly, and very efficient. Staff are welcoming and everyone seems to feel at home in this modest upstairs place, whether they're Persian or not! They hope to soon expand to another larger space. Maison du Kebab excels with its small and carefully-selected Persian menu!

# Malhi Sweets

**880 Jarry W.** (near Wiseman)
Métro: du Parc, then bus 80; or 179 from L'Acadie métro
Phone: 514.273.0407
Hours: 11am-11pm daily; closed Tuesday
Credit cards: cash only; Alcohol: beer and wine
Wheelchair access: entrance, yes; restroom, no
*Average main course: $7*

This Jarry Street resto serves delicious Sikh-style Punjabi food.

Some of the selections are unusual combinations so stretch your wings and enjoy yourself. The channa samosa appetizer is an unexpected pleasure, with a base of samosa pastry topped with a mixture of chickpeas, potatoes, green peas, onions, tomatoes, yogurt, and the whole thing finished with chutney. The lamb or goat curries are splendid and full flavoured. Butter chicken is a creamy and delicately-flavoured *tour de force*! Other good bets are the chicken tikka and the saag paneer spinach with mustard, onions and ginger. The dahl makhani is a great vegetarian choice of black kidney beans in a rich sauce of garlic, butter, and ginger, with an unusual spicy edge. There is a selection of nan bread and it pairs well with the food. No pork is served of course, and vegetarian dishes are available. One of the main attractions is the sweets, eat-in or take-out ($5/pound)—they have a great selection.

This family business began as a small dessert counter and it expanded into a full restaurant with sweets. Owner Burnamm Singh Malhi began with recipes from his wife and his mother, but there's a chef now and the food just seems to be getting better and better. Decoration has improved since their fire in 2003 with pastoral Indian scene wall hangings. A huge standing fan keeps things cool in warmer weather. Bollywood movies play on two satellite TVs (so everyone has a good view!) Kids are welcome and everyone loves the food, including Catherine Deneuve who celebrated her birthday here in February 2005.

# Maria Bonita

**5269 Casgrain** (at Maguire)
Métro: Laurier; or 55 bus (St-Laurent)
Phone: 514.807.4377
Hours: Mon-Sat 4pm-10pm; closed Sunday (phone ahead)
Credit cards: V, Interac; Alcohol: all
Wheelchair access: no
*Average main course: $11*

Maria Bonita serves authentic Mexican food in Mile End.

The good things start with smoky spicy salsa and light tortilla chips. For a main course you can order a full portion dish or several small ones. Pork quesadillas are lightly crisped tortillas filled with savoury shredded pork and cheese. *Sopes* have harmonious layers of black beans, cheese, sour cream, salsa, and lettuce. *Mole poblano* is excellent, pieces of chicken in a thick, rich sauce that is smoky, quietly spicy, with a strong chocolate taste. *Camarones al diabla* (spicy shrimp) and guacamole are favourites. Lamb *flautas* have a crisp wrapper and the filling is shredded lamb with a sprinkling of lemon. The dessert crepe is covered with a luscious, thick goat's milk caramel and topped with pecans—you really want to lick the plate! The food is authentic but there are dishes that are not very spicy (you can ask), so it's very approachable for even the timid palate, but some dishes are spicy and hot sauce is always available.

Maria Bonita (pretty Maria) is a bright and inviting place opened in December 2004 by chef Maria Chavez and Hector Veladiz from Mexico City. It's decorated with photos of Mexico and some folk art. Tablecloths are bright stripes and lighting is soft. Service is attentive, unobtrusive, and efficient. Some of the serving plates are beautiful terra cotta. The sidewalk terrace is pleasant—narrow with wooden flower boxes and tables with blue and yellow tiles. The whole scene comes together and rings true. When you need to get away from home on a small budget, Maria Bonita's food and atmosphere will take you on a little trip to Mexico.

# Marven's

**880 Ball Avenue** (at Wiseman)
Métro: Parc
Phone: 514.277.3625
Hours: Mon-Thurs 11am-11pm; Fri-Sat 11am-midnight;
   Sun 11am-11pm
Credit cards: no; Alcohol: all
Wheelchair access: no
*Souvlaki plate: $8.75-$9.75*

Marven's is all about Greek specialties in a friendly atmosphere.

One of the star attractions is the fried calamari (a half order for an appetizer or a full order for a feast). They're crisp perfection with a squeeze of lemon just as you pop them into your mouth. A half order of calamari with pikilia for one would make a perfect meal with lots of variety. Main courses include huge portions of charcoal-grilled meat and chicken and a selection of combos. The chops, shish kebabs, and seafood are at the edge of the Cheap Thrills guidelines but the servings are so large they can easily be shared. The meat is properly marinated before grilling. Most dishes are served with a mass of very fresh Greek salad with feta, fragrant Greek oregano and lemon, and large portions of rice *and* potatoes. You may want to pass on the frozen fries. Marven's is a great place for a few people or a large group. Order a few dishes and share it all family-style. Most people leave with a doggie bag. They have baklava but who wants dessert!

Marven's has been around since brothers Antonio and George Costopoulos bought a dépanneur from a man named Marven in 1975, and turned it into a Greek restaurant called Marven's. Their three children are now also involved. Grill staff have been here from the beginning—so by now they are masters! There's a moose head on the wall, the long tables are plain, it's often crowded and noisy, and there is no décor to speak of—but it all works anyway because you come to Marven's to feast on the good food.

# Mazurka

**64 Prince Arthur E.** (just east of St-Laurent)
Métro: Sherbrooke; or 55 bus (St-Laurent)
Phone: 514.844.3539
Hours: 11:30am-11pm daily
Credit cards: Interac; Alcohol: no
Wheelchair access: entrance, yes; restroom, no
*Specials with soup, main course, and beverage: $7.25-$8.25*

The Mazurka serves Polish comfort food and it's one of the best deals in town.

This is how your mom would cook if she were Polish. The special features pierogi, blintzes, potato pancakes, meat or vegetarian platter, or Polish sausages. At a bargain price the special includes great homemade soup and tea or coffee. Potato dumplings with plum or apricot filling and topped with butter or breadcrumbs are a very special treat, available only in summer. It's impossible to spend a lot of money here, even with à-la-carte specialties like Wiener schnitzel, salmon steak, chicken Kiev, osso bucco, or the perennial Mazurka favourite, goulash. Everything tastes like home cooking and portions are generous. Desserts are crème caramel, cakes, and cheesecake. Wine is available at very reasonable prices.

Stanislaw Mazurek opened the restaurant in 1952 on St-Laurent Boulevard, and it moved to its present location in 1964, amid plumbing and sandal shops. Now part of a trendy strip, it is run by Mazurek's daughter Josephine and her son Mark. The Mazurka "family" includes veteran servers like Grace (Stanislaw's daughter) who have been there for decades, as have many of the patrons. It is now a large establishment with 180 seats, two levels, and a terrace section. The atmosphere is still informal and relaxed, with folksy paintings of the old country on the walls. Service is friendly and extremely efficient.

# McKibbin's Irish Pub

**1426 Bishop** (bet. de Maisonneuve & Ste-Catherine)
Métro: Guy-Concordia
Phone: 514.288.1580
Hours: 11am-3am daily
Credit cards: V, MC, Amex, Interac; Alcohol: all
Wheelchair access: no
*Average main course: $9*

McKibbin's is a downtown Irish pub with all the trimmings, including excellent pub fare.

The food complements the bar offerings of course, but in the best pub tradition the food here is a real drawing card—not an afterthought. The kitchen pays attention to quality. The menu (in an old newspaper format) includes the story of the ghost of Mary Gallagher, old ads, a history of the red sandstone building itself, and other interesting bits. House specialties are Irish stew (with lamb), fish and chips, and burgers. The buffalo burger is a juicy, low-fat delight smothered in browned onions. Shepherd's pie and steak and kidney pie have savoury fillings enhanced by a flaky homemade crust. Chef Christophe Ritoux regularly features Cajun specialties like crab cakes and jambalaya. Set daily specials (salmon steak on Monday, prime rib or fried trout on Friday) or the chef's special are always a good bet. Fries are real, not frozen, and they're terrific. There are many imported beers and the house brew on tap, and you will also find a bountiful selection of single malt scotch.

Dean McKibbin and Rick Fon opened McKibbin's in 1997, but it feels like it's been there forever. It's all the things a good neighbourhood pub should be—warm, friendly, inviting, with good food and a well-stocked bar. A mix of Irish and contemporary bands plays in the evenings, and there's a very pleasant and secluded back terrace in summer. It's quite crowded for after-work drinks but not unpleasantly so. McKibbin's is a congenial and affordable downtown pub—where you can eat well!

# Melchorita

**7901 St-Dominique** (corner Gounod)
Phone: 514.382.2129
**6583 St-Laurent** (near Saint-Zotique)
Phone: 514.272.9449
Bus: 55 bus (Saint-Laurent) for both
Hours: Mon-Wed: 8.30am-10pm; Thurs-Sun 8:30am-midnight
Credit cards: V, MC, Interac; Alcohol: all
Wheelchair access: no
*Average main course: $10*

Melchorita serves Peruvian family cooking in the Little Italy part of town.

The portions are large, the food is fresh, simple, well cooked, and attractively presented. Be sure to ask for the hot sauce—it's a sublime flavour hit. The grilled chicken is delicious, moist and infused with a house marinade—you might want to pass on the frozen fries and go for the fried yucca instead. Mixed seafood platters (*jalea*) are large enough for two—deep fried fish and seafood served with great sauces and a superb marinated onion salad. Seafood soup (*parihuela*) is a massive bowl of lusty mixed seafood that will feed four. Potatoes are indigenous to Peru and they are important to the cuisine, so be sure to try them stuffed or with cheese. Fried squid is crisp and tender. Peruvian trucker-style breakfasts are an adventure, available daily 8:30 to noon, with fried pork, tamales, potatoes, bread, coffee, or hot chocolate.

Julia and Victor opened the main Melchorita in 1999 and the smaller Saint-Laurent location with a slightly more limited menu followed later. It's a family business and they proudly maintain the Peruvian food traditions with a warm and generous style. Service is friendly, knowledgeable, and competent. It's comfortable rather than classy, with tablecloths under glass, soft lighting in the evening, lots of wood and some Peruvian artifacts on the walls. You'll be tempted to bring a lot of people to Melchorita, order it all, and share some real Peruvian food, family-style.

# Mexicasa

**4118 St-Denis** (near Rachel)
Métro: Sherbrooke
Phone: 514.282.6418
Hours: 8am-midnight every day
Credit cards: V, MC, Amex, Interac; Alcohol: no
Wheelchair access: entrance, yes; restroom no
*Average main course: $10*

Mexicasa on St-Denis has real Mexican food at very affordable prices.

The food here may not be fine Mexican haute cuisine, neither is it Tex-Mex or a Canadianized version of Mexican food. It's simple, honest, earthy food. The tortilla soup is outstanding—a hearty soup with rich taste and pleasing texture and certainly not something you see much of around these parts. The guacamole is chunky with a bite, and it is served with tortilla chips and optional red beans. Flour tortillas with ham and cheese and salsa (*sincronizadas*) are good, but the quesadillas and the gorditas are exceptionally delectable with fillings of chicken, cheese, beans, or meat. *Tacos al pastor* (with pork marinated with pineapple) are also extremely good. Mexicasa offers various tacos, enchiladas, tostadas, and tamales, all made here from scratch. They also have some delightful and refreshing natural juices and Mexican soft drinks. There is flan or rice pudding for dessert. Mexican-style breakfast is served until 3 pm.

Yvonne Castillo opened Mexicasa in 2004 with the aim of presenting authentic Mexican food. She's a native of Mexico City and a former journalist. It's very much a family affair and her mother and father are often in the kitchen or out front. The restaurant is tucked into a small storefront and it's crowded but not uncomfortably so. There are wonderful whimsical wooden flower chairs brought from Mexico. They are extravagant and bright, and magically bring the Mexican sunshine to even a dreary Montreal winter day. The outdoor terrace is the place to be in good weather. Latino music adds to the agreeable atmosphere.

# Nguyen Phi

**6260 Côte-des-Neiges** (facing Kent Park)
Métro: Plamondon, then 161 bus, or 165 bus
Phone: 514.344.1863
Hours: 10am-10pm daily
Credit cards: Interac; Alcohol: beer only
Wheelchair access: no
*Average main course: $8 (prices include tax)*

Nguyen Phi serves great value Vietnamese food in Côte-des-Neiges.

The fresh shrimp spring rolls are so good you may want to bring them home for your own dinner parties—rice flour wrappers with a filling of vermicelli, mint, coriander, and shrimp with warm peanut sauce. Their Tonkinese beef soup is one of the best in town, served with crisp sprouts, lime, and hot chili to taste. Their grilled specialties (including brochettes, shrimp, chicken, beef, and pork) are generous and very nicely done—a nice touch for a Vietnamese restaurant. There are other items on the menu as well but the specialties of the house are definitely the soups and the grill. The combo meals are a good deal. There is homemade tapioca pudding for dessert.

Chef Nguyen Manh Thanh and his wife Loan Ho (she's out front) and chef Van Ho opened Nguyen Phi in 2003, after working in other restaurants. The décor in this second floor location is simple with some beautiful bonsai at the windows. It's not large and it gets very crowded at lunch, but is more relaxed in the evening. The daughters of the owners wait on tables and they are friendly and accommodating. Everything is kept spotlessly clean. Note that taxes are included in the prices. Nguyen Phil is a no-frills restaurant with enjoyable Vietnamese food.

# Nouba, La

**5280A du Parc** (near Fairmount)
Phone: 514.274.7436
Bus: 80
Hours: 10am-9pm
Credit cards: no; Alcohol: no
Wheelchair access: no
*Average main course: $12*

La Nouba is a Maghreb tea room and resto inside a used book store on Park Avenue.

The menu is very limited but the owners will do their best to accommodate your requests. An excellent brik with tuna and egg is available at all times. At lunch there are salads and a salad combo (carrot, chickpea, cucumber, grilled veggies, and tuna), or a sandwich made with mild Tunisian merguez, or with tuna, boiled eggs, and harissa. The sandwiches are a pleasant change from the norm and they are delicious. In the evening there is one main course that could be Tunisian couscous with lamb and veggies, fish kefta with tomato sauce, preserved lemon or lamb tagine, or couscous royal. The pastries are made in small batches in-house and they are as good as the best home-made: baklava, makroud (a buttery date-filled pastry), and hazelnut cream. Everything is made with a special touch—such as the carrot salad lightly perfumed with orange flower water. There is wonderful mint tea and good coffee.

Noura ben Achour was a Tunisian journalist who arrived in Montreal in 1991. She opened a wonderful little used bookstore in 2000 called *Au bon vieux livres*, with mostly French books, but also many picture books and a nice selection of used books in English. She started serving tea and coffee in 2001 and in 2004 she and her husband added sandwiches, salads, and a daily special. There are solid wooden tables and chairs, and a few lovely chairs and tables are out front on Parc Avenue in good weather. This is a great spot and a terrific concept—good food and used books!

# Om

**4382 St-Laurent** (near Marie-Anne)
Métro: Mount Royal, 55 bus
Phone: 514.287.3553
Hours: Tues-Fri 11:30am-3pm, 5:30pm-10pm; Sat-Sun 5:30 pm-10pm; closed Monday
Credit cards: V, MC, Amex, Interac; Alcohol: all
Wheelchair access: entrance, yes, with ramp; restroom, no
*Average main course: $8*

Om is a charming place on St-Laurent serving authentic Tibetan and Indian food.

Tibetan momos/dumplings (beef, vegetable, shrimp or sweet cheese fillings) are served with a mint dipping sauce. *Then thuk* soup is a meal in a bowl, with homemade noodles, vegetables, and chunks of chicken in a savoury broth—a truly wonderful dish that warms the body and the soul! Chili chicken comes with a rich sauce that's tasty rather than spicy. Beef with clear bean noodles has a light broth-like sauce imbued with wild mushrooms. Fried white bread sounds dreadful but what comes to the table is a delicious fougasse-shaped homemade bread that is fried golden brown with just a hint of sweetness—a splendid way to sop up the rich sauces. On the Indian side of the menu there is a fine butter chicken, biryanis, curries, and an unusual spinach and tofu dish. Desserts include fresh fruit with yogurt and rice pudding.

Tibetans Gerard Achod and Yanshen Lhamo (she's the cook) opened Om in 2003. Gerard, and his brother Sonam have food services experience and they are out front. The Achod family was in the first wave of 17 Tibetan refugees who came to Montreal in 1971. Yanshen arrived in 1984 to join the small community of about 120 Tibetans in Quebec. Tibet neighbours India, China, and Nepal, and has a long history of Buddhism. Om (named for the first syllable of the Tibetan Buddhist mantra) has a simple, elegant décor, with dark red walls, a wooden ceiling, dark wood tables and chairs, small colourful banners, and white tablecloths and napkins. We are fortunate these Tibetan Canadians are introducing us to the cuisine from this high altitude "Shangri La."

# Papa Khan

**1024 Jean-Talon W.** (corner l'Acadie)
Métro: L'Acadie; or 92 bus
Phone: 514.271.2711
Hours: 11am-11pm, closed Monday
Credit cards: Interac; Alcohol: no
Wheelchair access: yes
*Fried chicken: 2 pieces, $3.99; 4 pieces, $5.99; 10 pieces, $12.99*

Papa Khan on the Jean-Talon Asian strip is the place to go for delicious fried halal chicken or Pakistani snacks.

Fried chicken done to crisp perfection is Papa Khan's centre-piece. Accompaniments are very ordinary; frozen fries, coleslaw, salad. Fried chicken is juicy, tasty, *very* crisp—as good as it gets! All the chicken is fresh grain-fed, including, burgers, biryani and marinated wings seasoned with a house sauce available in regular, spicy and suicide. The extraordinary whole steamed chicken (one hour preparation, call ahead) is marinated, roasted, then steamed—it may just be some of the best chicken you've ever eaten! Don't overlook the Pakistani snacks—a culinary education to the uninitiated: nihari (long-cooked beef stew), dhahi badah (lentil donut with yogurt), chaana chaat (chickpea curry), shami kabob (beef and lentil kabobs), lahori chaana (chickpeas in gravy), and falooda (reduced and sweetened milk, with vermicelli and rose syrup—a cooling drink eaten with a spoon). Samosas have an especially fine filling of potato, peas, cumin, and secret ingredients. Snacks come with nan or roti and homemade fruit sauce. The frozen homemade kulfi (reduced milk with pistachios, almonds, and cardamom) is a delicious dessert. Everything is made in-house. There are family packs and Tuesday specials. They do a huge takeout business.

Humayoun Khan grew up in Ville LaSalle. There were no halal fast food places in Montreal and as a teenager when he went out with friends, he would only eat the fries at fast food restaurants. In 2003 (after McGill) he opened this halal fried chicken place in the old Logan's Bakery space. The atmosphere is charmless but that's no matter when the food is this good!

# Perle de Manila

**5839 Décarie** (near Van Horne)
Métro: Plamondon
Phone: 514.344.3670
Hours: Mon-Tues 2pm-9pm; Wed-Fri noon-9 pm;
    Sat-Sun 11am-9pm
Credit cards: cash only; Alcohol: no
Wheelchair access: no
*Weekend buffet: $7*

Perle de Manila serves authentic family-style Filipino cuisine on Décarie.

Real Filipino cooking is Southeast Asian—combining Thai, Malaysian, Spanish, and Indian sensibilities in true fusion cuisine. There is an unbelievably good weekend buffet that allows you to taste many dishes from the regular menu. *Pancit*, a traditional dish of transparent Thai vermicelli noodles, is stir-fried with crispy julienne vegetables flavoured with soy sauce. Depending on market availability, different vegetables are used and it turns out slightly different every time—always good! Filipino *Adobo* is tender stewed meat in a sauce that includes soy sauce and vinegar; the sauce flavours the accompanying jasmine-scented rice. Either chicken or pork *adobo* is a masterpiece! Vegetable dishes include *gulay*, *pinakbet*, and *diningdin* which combine squash, eggplant, green beans, leafy greens, and sometimes okra, bitter melon, and other veggies, stewed in their own natural juices. The result is clean and clear tastes in a light broth, each quite different depending upon the combinations. Delicious grilled BBQ pork skewers are one of the best bets of all. Hard-to-find *kilawan* is diced goat that is cooked then marinated and served cold as a munchie or appetizer. The fried tilapia is superb.

Owners Ricky Contaoe and Bibian and Raphael Dayo opened this little pearl in 2002 (in another spot), to provide home cooking to the Filipino community. In 2003 they moved to the present location. It's pleasant and group-friendly, with tablecloths and typical wicker plate holders. Service is warm and helpful. This wonderful Filipino food is authentic home cooking. It's different but somehow familiar. Be adventurous—come join the Filipino fiesta at Perle de Manila!

# Persepolis

**5700 Sherbrooke W.** (at Harvard)
Métro: Vendome, then 105 bus
Phone: 514.807.8747
Hours: Tues-Sun noon-9pm; closed Monday
Credit cards: no; Alcohol: no
Wheelchair: no
*Average main course: $11; sandwiches: $6.50-$10.50*
*(prices include tax)*

Persepolis is a small charming Persian brochetterie in NDG.

There is a lunch special during the week featuring reduced portions of regular menu items. The menu features a modest but interesting selection of kabobs and sandwiches. Everything is nicely spiced and perfectly charcoal grilled. The choice of meats includes filet mignon in two styles, chicken breast or leg, and ground beef. They also do grilled vegetarian kabobs. Generous combo dishes for two include soup or salad and saffron rice. Sandwiches feature the same grilled meats in a pita with lettuce, tomato, and Persian spices. Persian tea goes well with the food. There are no desserts but a small piece of Persian nougat with pistachio provides a sweet ending to the meal.

Amiable Hooshang Imanpour and his wife Deborah Riddle opened Persepolis in December 2004. He's an investment banker and this family business is a new endeavour. They redecorated completely. It is now a charming little place with a little sidewalk terrace out front that is quietly decorated with flowers—a pleasant place to view the Sherbrooke Street scene in good weather. The interior is tastefully decorated with the walls painted in soft, soothing colours. Tables are covered with cloths and then with a black plastic top that is quite elegant. The service is helpful, friendly, and efficient. Iranian music plays discreetly in the background. Persepolis is a pleasant place for Persian grilled food.

# Petit Verdun, Le

**5506 Verdun, Verdun** (corner Woodland)
Métro: Verdun, then 107 bus
Phone: 514.766.6669
Hours: Mon-Wed 11am-11pm; Thurs-Sat 11am-1am;
   closed Sunday
Credit cards: V, MC, Interac; Alcohol: all
Wheelchair access: yes
*10" sub with fries and salad: $8*

Le Petit Verdun serves steak subs, hand-cut fries, and charcoal grilled specialties.

The steak subs are wonderful concoctions overflowing with tender steak, nicely browned onions, mushrooms, peppers, salad, and other options if you prefer, all held together with melted mozzarella. Scrumptious! They come in three sizes, 5" (light meal), 10" (regular appetite), and 14" (big hungry!). An added bonus is that they come with fresh hand-cut fries perfectly cooked in canola oil—an occasional indulgence that's definitely worth the calories. Thin crust pizzas are also available, as are burgers and sandwiches. There is a chalkboard lunch special ($7-$8) with main course, salad and beverage that changes every couple of weeks. Delivery and takeout are very popular—those subs and pizza get around!

The amiable and enthusiastic Gary Karamanoukian bought the place in October 2004. He's a grad of Concordia and l'Institut de tourisme et d'hôtellerie with several years experience in food services and community work. He's slowly making over what was once a busy neighbourhood greasy spoon, while maintaining it as a local gathering place. He's adding charcoal grilled ribs, kebabs, and chicken. Staff is friendly and very accommodating. There are comfortable banquettes and an outdoor terrace out front with umbrellas. In the 17th century Verdun was a strategic fortification where Ville Marie residents took refuge during Iroquois attacks. It is now an interesting and changing neighbourhood with a wonderful waterfront promenade. Le Petit Verdun is aiming to grow and change with Verdun by providing an expanding selection of good food at good prices, and service with a big smile.

# Pharmacie Esperanza

**5490 St-Laurent** (at St-Viateur)
Bus: 55 (St-Laurent), or 80 (du Parc)
Phone: 514.948.3303
Hours: Tues-Sun 9am-1am, closed Monday
Credit cards: no; Alcohol: all
Wheelchair access: yes
*Average main course: $5*

Pharmacie Esperanza is a laid back vegetarian community café in Mile End.

Everything is vegetarian, and much of what is available is also vegan and organic. The breakfast burrito is very popular, or you can start the day with a choice of the special house granola with bananas (and either organic or soya milk or yogurt), tofu scramble, or an organic bagel with cream cheese or peanut butter. You are sure to find something that strikes your fancy among the 35 organic herbal teas, all grown in Quebec. They have put together some interesting combinations such as a sandwich of goat cheese, artichoke, olives, and spinach or brie with red peppers, both with a touch of Dijon mustard. The garlicky house mayo is great! There are daily specials. Weekend brunch is crepes with tea or coffee. Homemade cookies are good. The kitchen is committed to nutritious food that is also socially responsible, but they clearly want the food to be a pleasure too.

Pharmacie Esperanza is a feel-good place that has quickly established roots in the community. In 2003 Aimée Darcel set out to establish a place that offered healthy food, and a welcoming atmosphere that could also be used by a full range of community groups. The décor is earthy and well-worn with kitschy objects and art scattered through the large space that somehow manages to feel like an old-time country kitchen. It's relaxed, funky, the food, is good and it's a great place to hang out or to drop in for a community meeting or special event.

# Piment Fort

**8460 Lacordaire** (near Robert)
Métro: Cadillac, 32 bus
Phone: 514.326.5002
Hours: Mon-Fri 11am-2:30pm; 5pm-9pm; Sat 5pm-9pm;
  closed Sunday
Credit cards: V, MC, Amex, Interac; Alcohol: BYOB
Wheelchair access: no
*Average main course:* $10

Piment Fort serves Vietnamese and Chinese food in a small strip mall in St-Leonard.

Ingredients are always high quality and fresh and food is freshly prepared with no MSG used. Cold Vietnamese spring rolls with shrimp are great starters—unfailingly fresh and delicious, served with peanut or regular dipping sauce. Chicken dumplings are excellent, topped with rich and creamy peanut sauce. Tangy Szechuan tofu is a good vegetarian choice. Crispy fried noodles are topped with a generous helping of mixed vegetables and chicken or beef. Prawn dishes are made with prawns, not tiny shrimp. The food is not going to surprise you but it's reliably fresh home-style cooking rather than pre-packaged frozen restaurant portions. They do a huge amount of takeout and delivery in their area.

The Uong family started with a restaurant in Côte-des-Neiges but moved here in 1998; it's been a no smoking space since it opened in a small strip mall. Staff are friendly and personable without attitude here! There are comfortable booths as well as tables, large windows with distinctive café curtains, and flowered tablecloths. The décor is not intrusive and the lights are kept dim, but no so dim you can't see the food. Everything is kept spotlessly clean! It's a family place but it is not usually crowded since much of their business is takeout and delivery.

# Pizza Cachère Pita

6415 Décarie (near Plamondon)
Métro: Plamondon, or bus 160, 161, or 17
Phone: 514.731.7482
Hours: Sun-Thur 10am-10:30pm; Fri 10am-3pm (two hours before sundown); Sat: 1 hour after sundown-3am; closed all Jewish holidays (call ahead)
Credit cards: V, MC, Interac; Alcohol: no
Wheelchair access: entrance, yes; restroom, no
*Large falafel: $5.45; falafel plate: $8 (prices include tax)*

Pizza Cachère Pita is a frenetically busy kosher restaurant that serves fabulous falafel and other Middle Eastern staples in new digs on Décarie.

Falafel sandwiches here rival the best street food of Tel Aviv— large pita pouches stuffed to overflowing with falafel balls, red cabbage, lettuce, chickpea salad flavoured with cumin, cucumber, tomato, dill pickle, and a generous sprinkling of sumptuous fried eggplant, all dressed with tahina sauce and optional hot sauce. Eating falafel can be a messy business but who cares when it's this good! Order the falafel plate if you insist on being proper, but be warned it somehow doesn't taste the same when it's not dripping all over the place. There is no meat here, only dairy, so the pizza, hot dogs, and poutine are all vegetarian. They also have fish and chips, tuna melts, nachos, pasta, and eggplant parmesan. Pizzas are dressed to taste with olives, peppers, pineapple, artichoke, heart of palm, eggplant, tuna, and anchovies. They deliver all over town, but many people come just to do takeout.

Israeli-born Chaim and Tzvi Spiegelman keep the whole operation simple and fresh, making the food to order. You don't have to keep kosher to love the food here. They moved to their new space in 2004, and it has parking and the unforgettable Kosher Drive-Thru! The new space is larger but it can still be crowded and loud with lots of kids. It's great for late, late night snacks. They've got all the elements right and the food is delectable.

# Pizza Villa

**6672 Papineau** (near St-Zotique)
Métro: Papineau or Fabre, then 45 bus
Phone: 514.721.4711, 514.721.6072
Hours: Tues-Thurs 11am-midnight; Fri-Sat 11am-1am;
    Sun 4pm-midnight; closed Monday
Credit cards: V, MC, Amex, Interac; Alcohol: all
Wheelchair access: no
*Average main course: $9*

Pizza Villa is an old-time Italian restaurant that serves pizza, pasta, and submarines at reasonable prices on Papineau near Saint-Zotique.

Pizzas are great, baked crisp but not burnt and they don't stint with the toppings. They have all the expected fixings, but quite a few of their combinations include capicollo, a nice change. The 10" is a good size for a single diner and 12", 14" and 16" pizzas are for sharing. The pastas are cooked al dente, not turned to mush. The gnocchi are a special treat. Their basic sauce is real old fashioned Italian style, and it is not laced with Greek oregano and loads of sugar. Pastas can be baked in the oven with extra cheese for an additional $2.50. The eggplant parmesan is irresistible—they get it just right! Submarines are generous and the steak and capicollo combo is a good one. Pizza Villa also serve terrific bruschetta and that old favourite, *stracciatella Romana* soup. The veal and seafood dishes are outside the Cheap Thrills guidelines but they do them well if you want to splurge. There's a special menu for children ten and under.

Pizza Villa has been around since 1962, and was owned by Zuccheroso family from 1973 to 2004. It's now owned by chef Montuori and her husband Salvatore Montuori, with several family members involved. The place runs very smoothly and they are very accommodating. It's homey, decorated in rustic Italian style, and there are simple wooden chairs and tables. When you're tired of the trendy, and fed up with the food fads, head for this traditional Italian family restaurant of your dreams!

# Prato

**3891 St-Laurent** (near Napoléon)
Métro: Sherbrooke, or St-Laurent then 55 bus
Phone: 514.285.1616
Hours: Mon-Thurs 11:30 am-10pm; Sat 12:30pm-11pm;
    Sun 5pm-10pm (check in winter)
Credit cards: V, MC, Amex, Interac; Alcohol: all
Wheelchair access: yes
*Average main course: $10*

Prato serves terrific coal-fired brick-oven pizza on St-Laurent.

Although they serve good pasta, the main attraction here is the ravishing thin-crust pizza. At Prato pizza is served in its own large oblong baking pan and it's crisp in the way that only a coal-burning pizza oven can make it. This is worlds away from those ubiquitous 99 cent pizza points! Olive oil is brought to the table for an optional drizzle on the pizza—and you should do it! There is a plethora of topping combos and they maintain good balance between toppings, tomato sauce, and cheese. In addition to tomato-based pizza they have focaccia and a unique pizza bianca, with bacon, onions, rosemary, and crème fraîche. Salads are dressed with excellent vinaigrette. Vegetarian lasagna is a good bet if you're in the mood for pasta. There are lunch specials and they do some special things on weekends. They serve sangria, beer, and Italian wine.

Tony and Rosa Simonian opened Prato in 2000. They care deeply about food. Rosa makes everything market fresh from scratch (no frozen pizza dough here) with affection and attention, and it shows! Large windows look onto the ever-changing passing parade on St-Laurent. The ceilings are high and there are banquettes, and wooden tables and chairs. The large specially-built and non-polluting coal-burning pizza oven is visible. This is the only coal-burning pizza oven in Montreal— it's an Italian or New York City thing more than a Montreal thing—and some people swear it's the best way to bake a pizza. Check it out for yourself! Prato is deservedly popular. This fine food is also excellent value.

# Première Moisson

**1490 Sherbrooke W.** (near Mackay) plus 12 other branches
including in public markets and at Central Station
Métro: Guy-Concordia
Phone: 514.931.6540
Web site: www.premieremoisson.com
Hours: 7am-7:30pm; in summer they close at 8pm
Credit cards: V, MC, Interac; Alcohol: beer
Wheelchair access: no
*Daily special: $7.50*

This downtown French-style bakery café serves delightful light meals and extravagant pastries at very modest prices.

The special of the day includes a main course like beef bourguignon, quiche, salmon pie, or Provençal tart, salad, a light dessert, and beverage. They also serve a daily soup such as cream of vegetable. The sandwiches are on some of the best bread around—roast beef, bocconcini with pesto and tomato on olive bread, ham and cheese, and other charcuterie tasties. Don't overdose so you can indulge in the pastries. There are fabulous opéra cakes, mouth-watering fruit tarts, pear/almond tarts, millefeuilles, lemon tart, crème brulée, and a breathtaking array of other delights in the Le Nôtre style, including some delightful seasonal specialties. Everything is made fresh and it's all available to eat in or take out. Coffee is excellent and microbrewery beer is also available.

Première Moisson is a terrific bakery that grew and grew and grew—but it has found the magic recipe to rigorously maintain its high standards in all its locations. It is wildly popular and justifiably so. They also have an exquisite selection of house-made pâtés, quiches, and other French favourites. Other branches offer different possibilities and have different hours so don't expect that they are all exactly alike. The Sherbrooke Street branch has a delightful terrace that is ideal for people watching, morning, noon, and evening. Inspired breads, homemade charcuterie, fabulous pastries, good coffee, and prices you couldn't dream of in Paris. How can you go wrong?

# Pushap

**5195 Paré** (corner Mountain Sights)
**975 Jean-Talon W.** (near l'Acadie)
Métro: Namur/L'Acadie
Phone: Paré 514.737.4527; Jean-Talon: 514.274.3003
Hours: 11am-9pm daily (Jean-Talon is closed Monday)
Credit cards: cash only; Alcohol: no
Wheelchair access: yes (not Jean-Talon)
*Average main course: $6; thali $6*

Pushap is a wonderful bustling restaurant that serves home-style vegetarian Punjabi food.

They serve a full range of vegetarian dishes—and they're all great! The thali special of the day offers two choices of curry with dahl, rice, and one of several types of Indian breads, and it's always a good bet. They have what many think are the best samosas in town, served with tamarind sauce—utterly divine and addictive. The outsides are unfailingly crisp with potato/peas stuffing and the sharp bite of their own tamarind sauce. Homemade paneer goes into several wonderful dishes. Outstanding curries include potato/yam, and eggplant/tomato, but you won't go wrong with anything on this menu. Chapatis and parathas are ideal accompaniments. Spices are handled with a deft and knowing hand, and ingredients are fresh, fresh, fresh! Sweets are homemade and there are always at least a dozen choices, including milk cake, ladoo, barfi, and wonderful gajrela (carrot cake). Sweets are available for take-out at $4.50 a pound.

Daljit Mohan and members of his family look after the front. His mother and other family members produce the great Northern Indian vegetarian cuisine. There is no smoking. The Jean-Talon Pushap is also owned by Daljit and they do cook and swap. The West Island Pushap is a different operation owned by relatives. Pushap is always busy at peak times and the takeout line can be daunting. It can get harried but patience is well rewarded! You don't have to be vegetarian to like this food. Pushap is worth a special trip—this food is GOOD!

# Quartier Perse

**4241 Decarie** (corner Monkland)
Métro: Villa Maria
Phone: 514.488.6367
Hours: Mon-Thur 12pm-3pm, 5pm-10pm; Fri until 1:30pm
    Sat 5pm-11pm; Sun 5pm-10pm
Credit cards: V, MC; Alcohol: all
Wheelchair access: no
*Average evening special: $14*

This elegant NDG restaurant offers sophisticated Persian food.

The food is truly authentic and delightful unfamiliar dishes are home-style cooking done with flair and care. This place doesn't offer much choice for vegetarians. You can make up a tasty vegetarian meal from appetizers such as yogurt with wild Persian garlic, eggplant/tomato/garlic dip, an unusual but flavourful eggplant and whey dip, but the rest of the menu is for meat-eaters. The soup is wonderful and is almost a meal in itself. The daily special varies and it could include as a main course a wonderful beef stew with split peas and tomato rice, chicken stewed in a rich walnut and pomegranate sauce, or beef with kidney beans in a *fine herbes* sauce. The tender lamb shanks in a tangy lima bean sauce are excellent, as is the chicken breast marinated in lemon and saffron before grilling. Rice with tangy red Persian berries (*zershk*) is memorable! (*Zershk* are available in Middle Eastern groceries if you wish to try it at home.) It's fun to try things you've never eaten before, especially if they seem like unlikely combinations, and at Quartier Perse they always turn out so it's a double delight! The cooking is refined and the tastes are complex and interesting.

Mahin Kalantary is the owner-chef and her husband is the manager. They have created a tastefully decorated space with paisley tablecloths and discreet music. They had opened a branch on Sherbrooke near Royal but they have now sold it. There is a small and very pleasant outdoor terrace. Quartier Perse is a quintessential cheap thrill!

# Quatre Saisons

**4200 St-Jacques W.** (near St-Phillipe)
Métro: St. Henri
Phone: 514.932.3309
Hours: Tues-Sun 11am-10pm; closed Monday
Credit cards: Interac; Alcohol: all
Wheelchair access: no
*Average main course: $9*

Quatre Saisons in St-Henri specializes in Korean specialties cooked at the table.

Meals begin with six delicious appetizers to whet the appetite and amuse your palate before the main event. House specialties are Korean barbecue and shabu shabu. They bring a special cooker to the table for the BBQ, along with what you have ordered—beef, chicken, pork, tripe, or prawn. It can get a bit smoky but it's well worth it. Wrap the cooked meat in lettuce leaves and sauce and enjoy! This is good stuff! Shabu shabu was developed (so the story goes) by Genghis Khan to feed his troops quickly and efficiently. Bite-size pieces of meat/fish/seafood and veggies are swished by each diner in a "hot pot" of boiling broth until food is cooked to your taste. The final course is the soup which has become richer and tastier! They also serve spicy codfish soup, cold noodle soup with seafood, and spicy beef stew. The spicy dishes can be very hot, but you can request less heat. The menu includes Japanese dishes but most people stick with the Korean dishes. They have great lunch deals. Beautiful carved oranges for dessert are refreshing and complimentary.

Souk Soon Park opened this family business in 1998, and she is also the chef. She previously had a restaurant in Vancouver. Décor is not the strong point, but it's comfortable and casual, with really neat private booths for larger parties. There's a good feeling here, and ample room between tables. Staff are friendly, helpful, and attentive although language is sometimes a problem. This is some of the best Korean food in town and it's fun too!

# Riccardo's

**4071 St-Jean North** (near Lake)
Les Galeries St-Jean strip mall
Phone: 514.620.3477
Hours: Tues-Fri 11am-10pm; Sat-Sun 4pm-10pm
Credit cards: V, MC, Amex, Interac; Alcohol: all
Wheelchair access: yes
*Average main course: $10*

Riccardo's serves fresh pasta in homemade classic Italian sauces on the West Island.

They make their own cannelloni, manicotti, lasagna, and gnocci—always a treat. You can mix and match, your choice of pastas (spaghetti, penne, linguine, rigatoni, fettuccini, and stuffed pastas) can be ordered with excellent homemade sauces such as marinara, Bolognese, arrabbiata, rosée, Alfredo, puttanesca, and a really yummy red clam sauce. The manicotti is fresh pasta folded around a stuffing of creamy ricotta and spinach; it is then napped with sauce, and the whole thing is placed in the oven with cheese until it is fragrant and bubbling—really mouth-watering. All the pasta dishes are done well but the gnocci are soft and light—a very special treat available every day. Paninis are a popular choice for a light meal. Eggplant parmesan is one of the kitchen's strong points. It's beautifully balanced between cheese, eggplant, and tomatoes, no one element overwhelming the other, and everything coming together like a match made in heaven. Veal dishes are reasonably priced and they get raves, although they will take you a little beyond the Cheap Thrills guidelines. Pizzas are thick-crust and are popular with the kids. There is a good lunch special.

Sandra and Marco Intilli opened Riccardo's (named for a favourite uncle) in 2001. Their mother, Anita, is the cook—she's from the Marche but her husband is Sicilian so you get both sensibilities from this kitchen. The food is always nicely presented and service is excellent—fast, efficient, and friendly. There is a courtyard décor with arches, stucco, and stone walls. Riccardo's is about good food, reasonably-sized portions, and very good value for your dining dollar.

# Roi du Plateau

**51 Rachel W.** (corner Clark)
Bus: 55 (St-Laurent)
Phone: 514.844.8393
Hours: Mon-Sat 5pm-10:30pm; Sun 5pm-10pm.
  Reservations strongly suggested.
Credit cards: V, Interac; Alcohol: all
Wheelchair access: entranc,e yes, restroom, no
*Average main course*: $13

Roi du Plateau serves glorious Portuguese grill in the Plateau.

The menu contains nothing but Portuguese grill specialties, both seafood and meat. Everything is cooked fresh to order, portions are enormous, and there is not an item on this smallish menu that isn't delicious. Grilled squid is out of this world. The centrepiece at Roi du Plateau is the grilled chicken. It's moist and tender, perfectly spiced, smoky, and the skin is crisp and golden—a cut above the rest. The fries are wonderful. Pork with clams is a traditional Portuguese combo and if you've never tried it you're in for a treat. Shrimp, cod, clams, quail, pork, lamb—they're all grilled and all great. The grill guys are masters at what they do. Your only problem might be what you will not be able to choose. Vegetables are not a strong suit— a simple salad is as far as it goes. Vegetarians should try their luck elsewhere. Portuguese beer or wine goes really well with everything. They do *not* do takeout, preferring to take care of in-house customers properly in a limited space.

Monica and Michel Viegas came to Canada in 1970. He worked at Doval, and they opened this in 1997, with daughter Katia helping as well. They are very amiable and clearly happy that people enjoy themselves immensely here. It can get very busy and very noisy, and there are times when you just can't get in. It's not a fancy place, but it's perfect for a fun evening out rather than a romantic rendezvous. Every night a Latin guitar player/singer shows up and plays an eclectic mix of Latin songs and requests. Le Roi du Plateau is a real winner!

# Romados

**115 Rachel E.** (corner de Bullion)
Métro: Mont-Royal; or 55 bus
Phone: 514.849.1803
Hours: Mon-Wed 11am-8pm; Thurs-Sun 11am-9pm (bakery
 and butcher open at 6:30am)
Credit cards: cash only; Alcohol: grocery licence, but no
 drinking on the premises
Wheelchair access: yes (side door)
*Daily special: $7*

Romados includes a butcher shop, a bakery—and a charcoal grill that serves simple but exquisite Portuguese fare in the Plateau.

Frango chicken or pork is beautifully spiced with a wonderful sauce and charcoal grilled at the perfect height and angle so it is juicy yet crispy. There are also chicken or pork sandwiches (not available Sunday). Three daily specials include a main dish of meat, fish, or seafood such as crisp fried whole whiting, fried shrimp, or beef with vegetables. Plates or specials include fabulous fresh cut fries (double cooked in vegetable oil) or rice, a small salad, and a fresh bakery roll. Pick up a cold drink from the grocery section, and for dessert choose from the pastry counter! It couldn't be simpler. You can also buy a whole Frango chicken to take out.

Romados evolved from a butcher shop to a bakery, and they then expanded their rotisserie chicken operations into something much more substantial. There's still a small butcher counter (they make their own chouriços) and the spiffy new bakery counters display Portuguese bread and pastry specialties like the traditional custard tartlet *pastéis de nata*, coconut or lemon tart, and fancy cakes. But the main part of the business is now takeout or sit-down meals from the food counter and mini kitchen with full charcoal grill set up at the rear. Eating in is pretty basic with three tables with chairs and two counters with stools, but people continue to line up beside the frozen fish cooler for fresh and fabulous Portuguese grilled and fried chicken, meat, fish, and fries to eat here or take out.

# Rotisserie Mavi

**5192 Gatineau** (bet. Queen Mary & Jean-Brillant)
Métro: Côtes-des-Neiges
Phone: 514.340.9664
Hours: Mon-Wed 11am-10pm; Thur-Sat 11am-11pm;
   closed Sunday
Credit cards: cash only; Alcohol: all
Wheelchair access: 2 steps at entrance; restroom, no
*Average main course: $10*

Mavi serves perfect Portuguese charcoal-grilled meats and fish at amazing prices.

The specialty is grilled chicken, lovingly basted with home-made hot sauce and cooked over charcoal until it is smoky, crisp, and juicy. Depending upon how hungry or how greedy you are, choose a quarter, a half, or a whole chicken. Meals are served with fresh salad, and fries or rice. The fries are cut in-house and cooked in vegetable oil—really good. They also serve platters of Portuguese sausages, pork, beef, and ribs. Fish choices include cod, sardines, squid, shrimp, salmon, swordfish, and trout. Everything is grilled, everything is great! If you insist on the mundane, you can order a hamburger, but don't do it! Sumol is a refreshing Portuguese soft drink that is a good counterpoint to the food; they also offer six Portuguese wines, and an expanded selection of beer. You can order brandy and port, and there is still one lonely bottle of Johnny Walker Red Label on the shelf. But Mavi is more about eating fabulous grilled meat and fish than it is about drinking.

Maria Goa opened Mavi in 1997. She runs the place and husband João does delivery and helps out between runs in the evening and on weekends. They arrived from Portugal in 1987. Young son Michael is a cheerful presence. Mavi does a booming takeout and delivery business. They have painted and done some renovations but this is a very basic space and it can get smoky from the grill. Ah, but the food is something else altogether!

# Royal Sous-marines

**10 Bernard West** (near St-Laurent)
Bus: 55
Phone: 514.272.9788; 514.272.3520
Hours: Sun-Wed 11am-midnight; Thu-Sat 11am-1am
Credit cards: cash only; Alcohol: no
Wheelchair access: no
*Submarines: $6.75-$7.95*

Royal Sous-marines has been serving great submarines forever on Bernard near St-Laurent.

The big deal is the subs. They come in twelve variations, including the classic "Royal" with seared, thinly sliced steak, ham, pepperoni mushrooms, peppers and onions. There's also chicken, Greek style with feta and oregano, minced beef, and many others. The chewy bread soaks up the meat juices and the vinegary homemade sauce, and lettuce and tomato are mounded on top of the meat, open-face. Then the task becomes to somehow get the whole delicious mess into your mouth! They also serve perfectly respectable pizzas, souvlaki, and Greek salad, but at Royal the lure of the sub is strong—this is the place to eat subs, not pizza! Of course they deliver and do lots of takeout. Believe it or not this can be street food if you like— they wrap it tightly for takeout.

Owner John Tassis, a Greek immigrant, has owned Royal since 1982 but Royal has been selling submarines since 1950. It's totally non-décor with a few feeble decorations, an old counter with stools, six yellow tables and a wall of empty pizza boxes that separates the diners from the kitchen. There's an old black and white TV. This is a turn-back-the-clock neighbourhood sub joint with a Greek twist, and it's as comfortable and unpretentious as well-worn jeans! Long-time aficionados will drive a hundred miles to eat their favourite sub at Royal.

# Royal Sushi

**5011A du Parc** (St-Joseph)
Bus: 80
Phone: 514.274.5497
Hours: 11am-9pm daily
Credit cards: V, MC, Amex, Interac; Alcohol: no
Wheelchair access: no
*Average prices: sashimi $2.25; maki roll 6/$3.25, 8/$5.50;*
*futomaki cone $5*

Royal Sushi is a reliable but simple neighbourhood sushi shop on Parc Avenue.

This is not a trendy upscale sushi bar but the fish is never "off," the sushi is made to order, and it's all done well. The rice is lightly vinegared and the sushi don't fall apart when you dip. They use sesame seeds generously. Many combinations are available, and pickled ginger, soy sauce dip, and wasabi come on the side. The best bets are the tofu maki with peanut and ginger tofu, spinach, and homemade sauce. The West Coast maki is a familiar combination of smoked salmon, cream cheese, avocado, and fresh salmon. The végé-exotique maki combines daikon with Japanese market veggies, crispy tempura, and a creamy special sauce served on the side—delish! Imperial futomaki is a bit unusual and it's very good, combining cooked shrimp and chicken, teriyaki sauce, carrot and lettuce. Miso soup is available and they serve salads with a lovely creamy dressing. Takeout is popular.

Royal Sushi opened in 2004. You walk up a few stairs to a small square space with four black counters and stools. The décor is very particular with wall recesses with backlit vases of coloured water and artificial flowers—we are definitely not in a sushi chain here. Many people order to take out or help themselves to what's available in the fridge—it's always fresh, not carried over from yesterday. This may not be classically prepared high-end sushi as it is served in Japan but it's good North-American sushi. It's hard to find decent sushi at reasonable prices and this neighbourhood place is a very good bet for reliable sushi at a great price.

# Sablo Kafé

**50 St-Zotique E.** (at St-Dominique)
Bus: 55
Phone: 514.807.8241
Hours: Tues 9am-11pm; Wed 9am-9pm; Thurs-Sat 9am-11pm;
  Sun 9am-9pm; closed Monday; summer only, closed Sat and
  Sun at 5pm
Credit cards: cash only; Alcohol: all
Wheelchair access: no
*Average main course: $8*

Sablo Kafé serves an eclectic international menu in Little Italy,
and there are live performances on Tuesday and Friday evening.

The day starts here with substantial breakfast offerings,
including Moroccan eggs with warm tomato and red pepper
salad, eggs with feta and olives, and Asian/Indian eggs with
tomatoes and coriander chutney (*bou-bou*).  Sandwiches are
inspired combinations including smoked turkey with gouda
and pears, very good jerk chicken with roasted red pepper,
and tuna with curry sauce and mango chutney.  *Harira* is a
traditional Moroccan stew with chickpeas and dates, served
with cinnamon raisin bread. Excellent couscous is available
Tuesday and Thursday, and vegetarian curry is served on Wednesday. *Looz sharba* soup is a superb almond-based soup with
distinctive flavourings is great and they sometimes run out.
The jerk chicken is also available in a salad, as is the flavour-
packed tandoori chicken, and the dressing is very good.  Fresh
juice is a healthy accompaniment to this very sane menu.

Melanie Lalouz (she is Jewish) and Zohar Bardai (he is Muslim
from Zaire) are food lovers who love to cook and they opened
this place in 2002, indulging their love of many international
tastes.  It's bright, clean, spacious, and pleasantly spare with
wooden tables and chairs and changing artwork on the walls.
On Tuesday evenings, Kalmunity, an acoustic soul group with
live spoken word, takes the stage, and on Fridays there's live,
organic, improv-jazz/funk/reggae. Sablo Kafé is a fun place to
go to because the food is unfailingly good and the variety is
such that there's something for everyone, not to mention
interesting live performances.

# Saffron

**1801 Ste-Catherine W.** (at St-Mathieu)
Métro: Guy-Concordia
Phone: 514.937.7475
Hours: Mon-Thurs 11:30am-10:30pm, Sat-Sun 11:30am-2am
Credit cards: V, MC, Amex, Interac; Alcohol: all
Wheelchair access: yes
*Average meal: $12*

Saffron finally gives us a good Persian restaurant downtown!

The food is authentic and the meat is halal. Almost all dishes are beautifully flavoured with fine saffron—a word that comes from the Persian "za-fran". It's a pleasure to find good Persian vegetarian dishes. The *mirza ghashemi* is a delight—a large bowl of roasted eggplant, tomatoes, onions, garlic and spices. With rice—it could be a main course. The *borani*, yogurt and fresh spinach, is also an excellent vegetarian choice. *Zershk* chicken with barberries is a tangy delight. Marinated Crazy chicken is fit for an emperor's table. It features grilled chicken breasts with roasted tomatoes. Beef stew with parsley and spinach is nicely spiced. Most dishes include soup or salad and basmati rice, and the upper layer of rice is suffused with bright saffron colours. Don't overlook *doogh abali*, a sprightly yogurt beverage with soda and sea salt. Persian tea is served in the style of Abas Kiarostami films, in glasses, and with large cubes of sugar. The delicious twin dessert *zulbia* and *bamieh* is especially popular during Ramadan and it is delightfully perfumed with rosewater.

Hamid Mohammadian and partners Abbas and Raza opened Saffron in 2005. The impressive mural of Persepolis was painted by renowned Tehran artist Nasir Habib. Saffron is bright lue and yellow and decorated with impressive birds of paradise plants. On Fridays and Saturdays, starting at 11:30pm, there is a DJ and dancing. Saffron brings many Persian delights to downtown Montreal.

# St-Viateur Bagel & Café

**1127 Mont-Royal E.** (at Christophe-Colomb)
Métro: Mont-Royal, then 97 bus
Phone: 514.528.6361
Hours: 6am-11pm daily
Credit cards: Interac; Alcohol: all
Wheelchair access: yes
**5629 Monkland, NDG**
Métro:Villa Maria, then 103 bus
Phone: 514.487.8051
Hours: 6:30am-11pm daily
Credit cards: V, MC, Interac; Alcohol: all
Wheelchair access: yes
*Average bagel sandwich: $7*

The legendary St-Viateur bagel is also available on Mont-Royal East and Monkland—and it's gotten all dressed up!

St-Viateur's brick-oven-baked bagels are available to take out or to eat here. The hot item is bagel sandwiches served with choice of salad, and with a strategically-placed lettuce leaf so the filling doesn't slip through the middle! Selections include grilled chicken with cheddar, tuna melt with Swiss cheese, and traditional smoked salmon with cream cheese. These bagels are tender, slightly smoky, chewy, and utterly fresh. There is just a hint of sweetness from a quick pre-baking honey/water dunk. This is, after all, the quintessential Montreal bagel. Salads are generous, all ingredients fresh and top quality. Desserts are very good (especially cheesecake), supplied by Délices de Dawn and Kilo. Breakfasts are great with lots of choice.

Vince and Nick Morena started rolling bagels as teenagers. Vince made a deal with dad, Joe, owner of the landmark St-Viateur Bagel, to licence the name and recipe. He took two bagel makers with him in 1996 when he opened the café on Mont-Royal where centre-stage is a huge wood-burning brick oven in which some of the world's best bagels are baked. Soon he and his brother opened another on Monkland, where there's a great heated terrace out front. People love the food and the coziness of both places where you can linger over coffee. The bonus is you can also take home some warm St-Viateur bagels—Montreal's finest!

# Santangelo's Sandwicherie Italienne

**2350 Guy** (at Sherbrooke)
Métro: Guy-Concordia
Phone: 514.937.7444
Hours: Mon-Fri 11am-8pm; Sat 11am-6pm; closed Sunday
Credit cards: cash only; Alcohol: no
Wheelchair access: no
*Sandwiches: $5.25-$7.50; pasta: $8 (prices include tax)*

Yes!!! Real Italian sandwiches downtown—and Santangelo's has pasta too.

The main attraction is fantastic sandwiches! Porchetta, Italian sausage, veal roast, grilled chicken—they're all good but favourites are sausages made here and flavour-packed porchetta. They come with provolone cheese, lettuce, and tomato, hot peppers, or pickled eggplant. Everything is homemade: quality meat is cooked as you would do it at home, eggplant pickle is to die for, hot peppers are suitably zippy and tasty, and fabulous bread (especially the ciabatta) is from Lola's in St-Léonard. It's a dynamite combination! There are two sizes, a reasonable size on a Kaiser bun, and an oversize on ciabatta. They have salads too, including bocconcini or grilled chicken. They serve meat or cheese cannelloni (al forno), and a rotating daily pasta, all with their own tomato sauce. Pastas are from Mike and Dominic's Villa du Ravioli in Rivière des Prairies. Of course there's Brio, San Pellegrino, and Moca d'Oro Italian coffee. Cannoli are filled fresh on demand or you can have biscotti. Did we mention it was Italian?

Jon Carlo (JC) Santangelo from Laval opened here in December 2001, originally with a partner who made great sandwiches at his butcher shop. He's on his own now and following the business plan he developed in an entrepreneur class at Vanier College. It's a nice little place a few steps down on Guy at Sherbrooke, with a counter where you order your food and tables with comfortable chairs. No luxury, it's a sandwich place—but it's clean and comfortable. They do catering for offices or at home and they will deliver locally. It's a treat to find good Italian sandwiches and inexpensive pastas downtown!

# Schwartz's

**3895 St-Laurent** (near Duluth)
Bus: 55 bus
Phone: 514.842.4813
Hours: Sun-Thurs 8am-12:30am; Fri 8am-1:30am; Sat 8am-2:30 am
Credit cards: cash only; Alcohol: no
Wheelchair access: entrance yes; restroom no
*Smoked meat sandwich, fries, & soda: $7.70; steak & fixings, $13.95*

Schwartz's on the Main is Montreal smoked meat at its best—
maybe even Montreal at its best.

Schwartz's Hebrew Delicatessan is justly legendary for smoked
brisket that is juicy, tender, perfectly spiced. It tastes divine.
The classic meal choice is a sandwich, fries, and a dill pickle,
washed down with a black cherry soda. Medium (fat) has the
perfect proportion of fat to lean. Sandwiches are made of
piping hot, expertly hand-cut meat piled high on fresh
sourdough rye bread. Fries are freshly made, cooked perfectly
in vegetable oil. Pickles are Mrs. Whytes—try the half sours.
Smoked meat platters are available for those who don't want
to do the sandwich juggle, but they're huge and definitely less
fun! There's an open charcoal grill and they charbroil a terrific
rib steak with a small side order of liver and a frank if you are
feeling ravenous. You can take out sandwiches, cold and hot
meat by the pound, or smoked chicken. Smoked ducks and
turkeys can be ordered for holidays. The smoking and spicing
are faultless, and it's all done without preservatives!

Schwartz's still has an old-time deli atmosphere all its own—
narrow and cramped with barely enough room to move. There
are often long lineups (even for takeout) but it's worth the
wait even if it's snowing and blowing. Staffed by veteran waiters,
service is efficient and there's no attitude. The distinctive
Rumanian-style smoked meat has become known as "Montreal" smoked meat, the standard against which all others are
measured. It's often brought to far-flung parts of the world to
provide expats and one-time visitors with a Montreal fix. IT
DOESN'T GET ANY BETTER THAN THIS!

# Shish-Kebab

**9394 Blvd. de L'Acadie** (near Chabanel)
Métro: L'Acadie, then 179 bus
Phone: 514.858.6222
Hours: 11am-11pm daily
Credit cards: V, MC, Interac; Alcohol: all
Wheelchair access: yes
*Average grill platter: $11*

Restaurant Shish-Kebab near the Marché Central has excellent grilled Lebanese kebabs and other specialties.

All the grill platters include salad, hummus, rice or fries, and pita bread. Portions are huge and can be shared. The tasty filet mignon shish kebab platter is a real winner (two or three kebabs). They are even better as leftovers in a sandwich! Shish taouk and ground meat kebabs are neither undercooked nor dried out. There is an interesting fish tagine appetizer. Tiny homemade Lebanese sausages cooked in lemon are outstanding! Hummus is faultless, and the smoky, silky baba gannouj may just be the best in the city! Vegetarian options include some interesting cheese specialties. Fries are hand-cut on site and fried in canola oil—lovely! Grilled meat sandwiches are an option for a lighter meal. Small whole onions grilled kebab-style are a nice touch. There are great lunch specials. There's baklava of course for dessert. They have pizza and burgers but almost everyone ignores them for the grilled goodies.

Toufic Nakhoul and his wife Françoise emigrated from Lebanon in 1999 with his parents. He had a restaurant in Lebanon for six years and opened Shish-Kebab in 2000. It's a family operation with everyone involved cooking, serving, and hosting. The mother cooks, and the brother does the grill. It's spacious with lots of light, free parking in front, and they're always working at upgrading the interior. They do takeout and delivery. They're open late and it's good choice after working late on nearby Chabanel or after shopping at Winners, Club Price, or Réno-Dépôt just across L'Acadie. This is a perfect food stop for great grilled kebabs and that memorable baba gannouj!

# Strega du Village

**1477 Ste-Catherine E.** (at Beaudry)
Métro: Beaudry
Phone: 514.523.6000
Hours: Mon-Fri 11am-midnight; Sat-Sun 4:30pm-midnight
Credit cards: V, MC, Interac; Alcohol: all
Wheelchair access: yes
*Average table d'hôte (including soup or salad, main course, and beverage): $11*

La Strega du Village is a charming resto for a wonderful Italian meal in the Gay Village.

Combine your choice of al dente homemade pasta with any of the fine sauces. Choices include arabbiata, Alfredo, pesto, red or white clam, puttanesca, and matriciana. Lasagne, manicotti, cannelloni, and tortellini are also available. Add sausages, artichokes, mushrooms, or smoked salmon for a small premium. Pastas are always cooked to order, and the quality is consistent, with fresh parmesan added to taste. Gigi with prosciutto, mushrooms, and white wine is a house specialty. The table d'hôte includes some pasta dishes, fish, and meat choices. Veal choices are excellent and the prices are unheard-of elsewhere. Salad is fresh with a house dressing. Appetizers are wonderful and can be put together for a meal. This isn't exciting and trendy food: they consistently produce quality versions of standbys like pasta arabbiata, beef Bourguignon, and veal with mustard sauce. There are no nasty surprises—quite the reverse, given the modest prices.

Antonio Kelada (a native of Calabria) had a resto in Genoa before he came here in 1980. He opened the wonderful L'Amalfitana in 1986 near Radio-Canada and sold it in 2000. In 2000 he renovated an old fast food place and opened here. It's intimate, with old-fashioned charm, red walls, cloth tablecloths, and an eclectic choice of Italian background music. But most important, Antonio is in the kitchen! They are accommodating and service is efficient, although it slows down at peak times. We can thank Antonio for offering his wonderful food at such affordable prices!

# Tabaq

**149 Jean-Talon W.** (at Waverly)
Bus: 55 (St-Laurent) or 92 (Jean-Talon)
Phone: 514.277.9339
Hours: 11am-11pm, closed Tuesday
Credit cards: Interac; Alcohol: no
Wheelchair access: no
*Average main course: $7*

Tabaq offers exciting Pakistani/Punjabi food on Jean-Talon near St-Laurent.

Each dish at Tabaq has its own distinct spicing—food is not made from an all-in-one curry paste. They serve authentic Pakistani cooking with some fresh tastes that aren't found elsewhere in Montreal restos. The meat is halal, they serve no pork, and they offer an extensive selection of vegetarian dishes. Some of the food is uncompromisingly hot so check about spice levels if you have a preference. The nan bread is chewy, light and puffy, great for scooping up the delightful gravies, with nice garlic or cheese variations. The butter chicken is a fabulous creamy delight, not too spicy. Tandoori chicken is terrific—moist and tasty, served in pieces that are golden rather than the red we usually see. Lamb or goat curries and biryanis are all delicious. The paneer and okra dishes, and the vegetable biryani are all good vegetarian choices. Lassi (sweet, salt, and mango) and raita are wonderful counterpoints to the food. They do a special weekend breakfast. For dessert there is gulab-jaman, kheer, or Qasuri Faloda ice cream. They do catering, takeout and delivery.

Owner Ahmed Asif had restaurants in Pakistan before he opened Tabaq, first on nearby Ogilvie then in this location in 2004. He is a young, enthusiastic, and talented chef. The restaurant has two sections, a casual diner-type space with banquettes and a more elegant spacious part set with tablecloths. It's low-key, friendly, and staff are happy to explain things. Be sure to reserve on weekends, they often do private parties. Tabaq means a platter of beautiful food and that's exactly what you get here!

# The Main

**3864 St-Laurent** (near Duluth)
Bus: 55 (St-Laurent)
Phone: 514.843.8126
Hours: 10am-5am daily; closed Christmas Day
Credit cards: V, MC, Amex, Interac; Alcohol: wine and beer
Wheelchair access: no
*Rib steak and fixings: $14*

The Main is a popular old-time steak house and deli that's open late on St-Laurent.

The two most popular meals are charcoal grilled steak and smoked meat sandwiches. They also serve very good chopped liver, and now have marinated grilled ribs (baby back and beef). There's a lovely 14-ounce rib steak with all the fixings (liver and frankfurter appetizer, coleslaw, pickle, French fries)—a steal at $13.95. It's hard to compete with Schwartz's across the street but they make their own Montreal-style smoked meat— and it's really good. Fries are excellent, fresh cut and double fried in canola oil! They serve matzo ball soup and many other deli delights—all well done. Desserts are something of an after-thought..

Peter Varvaro bought Kravitz's Steak House in 1974. He changed the name to The Main and started making his own smoked meat to compete with nearby Schwartz's. He moved across the street in 1984 to the present location. The Varvaro family has been serving Montrealers for decades. Peter and his father and brother owned the famous El Morocco nightclub in the 1960s, and his son is the Pete of Pete's Smoked Meat.

The Main has a good deli/steakhouse feel, with comfortable banquettes and nothing chichi about it. You come here to eat good food in a relaxed and unhurried place, to socialize with longtime staff or regulars if you wish, or to pick up the $15 family takeout pack that includes smoked meat, coleslaw, potato salad, latkes, pickles, rye bread and chopped liver—a real deal! The Main is an old-time deli/steakhouse and it's a good bet into the small hours of the morning.

# Tropico, Le

9153 **Pie-IX** (corner 47th St.)
Métro: Pie-IX, then bus 139
Phone: 514.327.4554
Hours: 11am-11pm
Credit cards: V, MC, Interac; Alcohol: no
Wheelchair access: entrance, yes; restroom, no
*Average main dish*: *$9 (prices include tax)*

Le Tropico is a Haitian hot spot way up north on Pie-IX.

Grillot (or griot) is a signature Haitian dish and they do a spicy and tasty version with boneless cubes of grilled marinated pork. The patties have a flaky pastry and savoury chicken filling. Most dishes can be ordered fried or in sauce. The red snapper is an extra large portion of meltingly-tender whole fish in a sumptuous sauce. They have goat, chicken, stew, turkey, and conch. Everything is prepared well, respecting the basic qualities of the fresh ingredients, and not masking the food with a long list of extra ingredients. Hot sauce on the side has a mellow heat. Dishes are served with traditional rice and beans, twice-fried plantains, and a small green salad. Fresh tropical juices add a perfect touch. This is authentic Haitian cooking, with all the tastes of Créole cuisine. In almost all dishes you find lime juice, sour orange, and hot peppers among the layers of flavour.

The Charles family opened Le Tropico in 1998 and they run the kitchen with a sure and steady hand. They serve authentic Haitian home cooking—they don't take flights of fancy into new territory. The décor is basic but it's comfortable with table-cloths, bistro chairs, plants, mango-coloured curtains, and lots of light coming through the windows. It's non-smoking. Take-out is a large part of their business, and they deliver and cater too. This is Créole home cooking up north!

# Vasco de Gama

**1472 Peel Street** (near de Maisonneuve)
Métro: Peel
Phone: 514.286.2688
Hours: Mon-Wed 7am-7pm; Thurs-Fri 7am-9pm;
   Sat-Sun 9am-6pm
Credit cards: V, MC, Interac; Alcohol: wine and beer
Wheelchair access: no
**1257 Bernard** (514.272.2688)
*Average sandwich and salad: $11*

Vasco de Gama is a chic downtown sandwich outpost for the formidable Ferreira next door.

For breakfast they serve a variety of light breakfast choices like cottage cheese with fruit or toasted baguette with jam, as well as omelettes. There is a salad, a soup, and a sandwich of the day—always good choices. Sandwiches are splendid, with real food and inspired combinations, not cardboard fillings. Choices include magnificent suckling pig, Quebec veal, lamb confit with caramelized onions. Vegetarian panini taste like a Mediterranean garden in late summer: excellent olive bread with grilled eggplant and mushroom, tomato tapenade, creamy goat cheese, and a sprinkling of fresh rosemary. It's hard to choose because everything is outstanding and of impeccable quality! They serve great tapas (codcakes, shrimp, *jamon*) in the evening. For dessert try the creamy light tart, traditional Portuguese *pastéis de nata*. Illy coffee is divine, as always. They have luxurious port and champagne by the glass!

Carlos Ferreira opened Vasco de Gama in 2004. He started with the Van Houtte on McGill College in 1990 then he opened the hugely successful Ferreira next door in 2002. There is a second café on Bernard, same idea but different hours and menu. All have offered excellent quality, service, and value. This space is intimate and in quiet good taste with comfortable banquettes, small tables, and plush stools. Old World maps are reminiscent of Portuguese explorer Vasco de Gama who discovered the water route from Europe to India. This is not the place to come for a quick bite on the run—this is fabulous slow food, so take the time to linger and enjoy!

# Villa Wellington

**4701 Wellington, Verdun** (2nd Ave.)
Métro: De l'Eglise; or 58 or 61 bus
Phone: 514.768.0102
Hours: Tue-Sun 11am-10pm; closed Monday
Credit cards: V, MC, Interac; Alcohol: all
Wheelchair access: yes
*Seafood platter for two: $20*

It's worth the trip to Verdun for this Peruvian restaurant.

Potatoes are native to Peru and Peruvians are very partial to them. The menu includes many different kinds of potatoes— all deliciously prepared. The daily soup is a substantial dish and a good buy. Daily specials are a good bet and a great buy. Starters include a stuffed potato, soft and fragrant tamales, and boiled potatoes with a cheese sauce. Main dishes for the specials include marinated chicken, beef stew with coriander, and fried pork. There are also many à la carte dishes such as ceviche, seafood soup, grilled fish, delicious fried squid, and grilled trout. Peru has a long coastline on the South Pacific Ocean and seafood is an important part of the cuisine. The heaping fried seafood plate (enough for two) is so wonderful it defies description! There is also a choice of non-Peruvian dishes, basic Italian and Greek food, but it's best to ignore them and go for the Peruvian specialties they do so well and that you can't get elsewhere. Forget the desserts, you won't have room anyway, platters are full to overflowing! Corona beer goes very well with the Peruvian specialties. They do takeout but do not deliver.

The décor is Peruvian, with hand-woven tablecloths under plastic, and paper placemats—nothing fancy. This is a neighbourhood family restaurant and although the staff is Latin, the clientèle is mixed. Latin music adds to the good feeling about the place. Peruvian owners August Saravia and Lise Ramirez live in Verdun. They opened the restaurant in 1992 offering no-frills food at bargain basement prices. You'll enjoy the food here, especially the seafood and the potatoes!

# Village Mon Nan

**1098 Clark** (near René-Lévesque)
Métro: St-Laurent or Place d'Armes
Phone: 514.879.9680
Hours: 11am-11pm daily
Credit cards: V, MC, Amex; Alcohol: all
Wheelchair access: no
*Peking duck (for three): $35*

Village Mon Nan in Chinatown specializes in exquisite Peking duck available at all times, without pre-ordering.

The menu contains a whole range of Peking and Shanghai style dishes, and the kitchen does them well, but the Peking duck is so tempting that it's hard to order anything else. The duck is served in three delicious courses. The first course is duck sliced thin with crispy skin intact, ready to be rolled up in small paper-thin warm pancakes with scallions and hoisin sauce. That taste is unforgettable! The second course is a duck and vegetable stir-fry. Be sure you get the finale—duck soup with thin clear noodles. The duck dinner feeds three comfortably. You might want to order steamed rice to go with it. If you are four, you can stretch it by starting with their delicious steamed or fried dumplings, or whatever strikes your fancy from the menu. Now you can order a half duck, or you can order two ducks, but you'll probably need a doggie bag as well.

This is a pleasant resto upstairs from the Mon Nan, which serves Cantonese food. John Lee manages both. Peking duck master chef Chef Ye does it all. Service can sometimes be a little offhand. When a craving for Peking duck hits, this is the place to go!

# The Sex of Restaurants

## Josh Freed

There is no task more daunting to the average anglo than making a restaurant reservation—the ultimate cultural survival test.

In Ontario, any fool can make a reservation—you must open the phone book and look up your restaurant. But in Quebec, you must first know the *sex* of your restaurant.

Let's say you want a reservation at a little place you heard about from some friends—the Viaduc restaurant.

But is it masculine: le Viaduc? Or feminine: la Viaduc? Or could it be listed under something tricky—like Le Restaurant La Viaduc?

It's not easy to remember your genders when you're standing in a phone booth, in −34°, with your gloves off. And even when you consult your pocket dictionary and find that Viaduc is masculine, your search has just begun.

Is it Restaurant Le Viaduc, or Restaurant du Viaduc? Restaurant les Viaducs, or Restaurant des Viaducs? All are grammatically correct.

It could also be listed under Restaurant Chez Viaduc or Restaurant Chez le Viaduc (over 100 restaurants are listed under Chez alone.) Not to mention Restaurant au Viaduc, Restaurant aux Viaducs or Le Restaurant aux Viaducs.

Get one pronoun wrong and you eat at home.

And who's to say the Viaduc is actually classified as a restaurant? It might be listed as a café, and if so, is it a café-restaurant or a restaurant-café?

Or could it be something trendy, like a café-terrace? Each of these have separate listings—hundreds of pages apart.

You don't believe me? Check the Montreal phone book. There are listings for restaurant-bars and bar-restaurants. For restaurant-bistros and bistro-cafés, There are restaurant-charcuteries, restaurant-patisseries, restaurant-pizzerias, and restaurant-brochetteries.

Not to mention brochetterie-restaurants.

It's not easy being an anglophone on the telephone. Or afterwards. Because once you've found your restaurant and showed up for your reservation, you still have to order.

Hmmm—now what's the sex of Caesar salad?

From *Fear of Frying and Other Fax of Life* by Josh Freed. Winner of the Stephen Leacock Prize for Humour. Published by Véhicule Press.

# Specialty Index

**Asian Fusion**
Bo 15
Chino Soul 51
Soy 18

**Bakery Restos**
Olive & Gourmando 17
Première Moisson 86
Romados 92

**BBQ**
Chalet Bar B-Q 45
Romados 92

**Bistro**
Bistro Gourmet 2 15
Bistro San Lucas 32
Cluny Artbar 16
La Cabane 38

**Brew-pub**
Réservoir 18

**Burgers/submarines**
Banquise, La 28
L'Exception 57
Petit Verdun, Le 80
Pizza Villa 84
Royal Sous-marines 94

**BYOB**
Amelio's 21
Ban Lao Thai 26
Lin et Lin 60
Piment Fort 82

**Café**
Brodino 15
Café L'Étranger 40

Café Titanic 16
Caffe Grazie Mille 42
Cobalt 53
Gourmets Pressé, Les 17
MbCo 17
Olive & Gourmando 17
Première Moisson 86
Sablo Kafé 96
St-Viateur Bagel & Café 98
Vasco de Gama 106

**Caribbean**
Caraibe Delite 43
Chino-Soul 51
L Corridor 59
Ma's Place 64

**Chilean**
Chilenita, La 50

**Chinese**
Buffet Palace Orientale 37
Lin et Lin 60
Piment Fort 82
Village Mon Nan 108

**Cuban**
Cuba 55

**Deli**
Schwartz's 100
The Main 104

**Diner**
B&M 25
Binerie Mont-Royal, La 31
Banquise, La 28

**French**
Bistro Gourmet 2 15
Grand Comptoir, Le 17

**Greek**
Bistro San Lucas 32
Diogènes 56
Marven's 69

**Guyanese**
Caraibe Delite 43

**Haitian**
Tropico, Le 105

**Hungarian**
Café Rococco 41

**Indian**
Bombay Choupati 34
Bombay Mahal 35
Malhi Sweets 67
Om 76
Pushap 87

**Iranian**
Maison du Kebab 66
Persepolis 79
Quartier Perse 88
Saffron 97

**Irish**
McKibbin's Irish Pub 71

**Israeli**
Chez Benny 47
Pizza Cachère Pizza 83

**Italian**
Agostini 19
Amelio's 21

Beniamino & Co 30
Café International 39
Pizza Villa 84
Prato 85
Riccardo's 90
Santangelo's Sandwicherie
  Italienne 99
Strega du Village 102

**Korean**
Arirang 22
Chez Bong (Chinatown) 48
Chez Bong (Downtown) 49
Quatre Saisons 89

**Kosher**
Chez Benny 47
Pizza Cachère Pita 83

**Laotian**
Ban Lao Thai 26
Lobby Bar 61

**Late night**
B&M 25
Banquise, La 28
Cabane, La 38
Café International 39
Chino-Soul 51
McKibbin's Irish Pub 71
Schwartz's 100
The Main 104

**Lebanese**
Shish Kebob 101

**Maghreb**
Nouba, La 75

**Moroccan**
Chez Badi 46

Maison du Bedouin 65

**Mexican**
Chilenita, La 50
Maria Bonita 68
Mexicasa 73

**Pakistani**
Papa Khan 77
Tabaq 103

**Peruvian**
Melchorita 72
Villa Wellington 107

**Philipine**
Perle de Manila 78

**Pizza**
Pizza Cachère Pizza 83
Pizza Villa 84

**Polish**
Chopin 16
Cracovie 54
Mazurka 70

**Portuguese**
Barroso Grill 29
Braseiro 36
Roi du Plateau 91
Romados 92
Rotisserie Mavi 93

**Québécois**
Banquise, La 28
Binerie Mont-Royal, La 31
Chez Clo 16

**Romanian**
Boite à Lunch 33

**Rotisserie**
Chalet Bar B-Q 45

**Russian**
Caverne, Le 44

**Salvadoran**
Los Planes Pupuseria 63

**Senegalese**
Keur Fatou 58

**Steaks**
Schwartz's 100
The Main 104

**Sushi**
Royal Sushi 95

**Takeout**
Beniamino & Co 30
Chez Benny 47
Chilenita, La 50
MbCo 17
Papa Khan 77
Petit Verdun, Le 80
Pizza Villa 84
Première Moisson 86
Romados 92
Royal Sous-marines 94

**Thai**
Ban Lao Thai 26
Bangkok 27
Chino-Soul 51
Chuch 52

**Uyghur**
Arzou Express 23

**Vegetarian**
Aux Vivres 24

Chuch 52
Lola Rosa 62
Pharmacie Esperanza 81
Pizza Cachère Pita 83
Pushap 87

**Vietnamese**
Nguyen Phi 74
Piment Fort 82

**Yemenite**
Al Mandy 20

# Neighbourhood Index

**Atwater**
Maison du Kebab 66

**Centre East**
Banquise, La 28
Cuba 55
Exception, L' 57
Strega du Village, La 102

**Chinatown**
Chez Bong 48
Village Mon Nan 108

**Côte-des-Neiges**
Arzou Express 23
Caverne, La 44
Chez Benny 47
Chino-Soul 51
Cracovie 54
Nguyen Phi 74
Perle de Manila 78
Pizza Cachère Pizza 83
Rotisserie Mavi 93

**Downtown**
Al Mandy 20
Arirang 22
Bangkok 27
Café L'Étranger 40
Café Rococo 41
Chez Badie 46
Chez Bong 49
Grand Comptoir, Le 17
Maison du Bedouin 65
MbCo 17
McKibbin's Irish Pub 71
Première Moisson 86
Saffron 97

Santangelo's Sandwicherie
    Italienne 99
Vasco de Gama 106

**Jean-Talon/Décarie**
Pushap 87

**Lasalle**
Buffet Palace Oriental 37

**Little Italy**
Café International 39
Melchorita 72
Sablo Kafé 96
Tabaq 103

**Marché Central/L'Acadie**
Shish-Kebab 101

**McGill Ghetto**
Amelio's 21
Lola Rosa 62

**Mile End**
Caffe Grazie Mille 42
Caraibe Delite 43
Keur Fatou 58
Maria Bonita 68
Nouba, La 75
Pharmacie Esperanza 81
Royal Sous-marines 94
Royal Sushi 95

**Montreal North**
Piment Fort 82
Tropico, Le 105

**NDG**
Agostini 19
B&M 25
Boîte à Lunch 33
Chalet Bar B-Q 45
Chopin 16
Ma's Place 64
Persepolis 79
Quartier Perse 88
St-Viateur Bagel & Café 98

**Old Montreal**
Beniamino & Co. 30
Café Titanic 16
Cluny 16
Cobalt 53
Gourmet Pressés, Les 17
Olive & Gourmando 17

**Ontario East**
Barroso Grill 29
Chez Clo 16

**Outremont**
Brodino 15

**Park Extension**
Bombay Mahal 35
Malhi Sweets 67
Marven's 69
Papa Khan 77
Pushap 87

**Plateau Mont-Royal**
Aux Vivres 24
Binerie Mont-Royal, La 31
Bistro Gourmet 2 15
Bo 15
Cabane, La 38
Chilenita, La 50
Chuch 52

L Corridor 59
Lobby Bar 61
Mazurka 70
Mexicasa 73
Om 76
Prato 85
Reservoir 18
Roi du Plateau 91
Romados 92
St-Viateur Bagel & Café 98
Schwartz's 100
Soy 18
The Main 104

**Pointe St-Charles**
Bistro San Lucas 32

**Rosemont**
Lin et Lin 60
Los Plaes Pupuseria 63
Pizza Villa 84

**St-Henri**
Gourmets Pressés, Les 17
Quatre Saisons 89

**St-Léonard**
Piment Fort 82

**Verdun**
Petit Verdun, Le 80
Villa Wellington 107

**Villeray**
Braseiro 36
Melchorita 72

**Ville St-Laurent**
Ban Lao Thai 26
Chez Benny 47
Diogènes 56